THE FIRST BOOK OF THE ANVARI SUHELI

THE FIRST BOOK OF THE ANVARI SUHELI

A LITERAL TRANSLATION IN ENGLISH

RUDYARD KIPLING

GYAN

Published by

GYAN

Gyan Publishing House
5, Ansari Road
Daryaganj, New Delhi-110002
Phone: 011-47034999, 9811692060
E-mail: books@gyanbooks.com

Distribution Network
gyanbooks.com
India, USA, Canada, UK, Australia

ISBN: 978-93-7169-085-0 (PB)

First Published, 1835

2nd Impression 2025

Printed at: Gyan Press, Delhi.

THE FIRST BOOK OF THE ANVARI SUHELI
Author: HENRY GEORGE KEENE

THE

FIRST BOOK

OF THE

ANVĀRI SUHELĪ,

A LITERAL TRANSLATION IN ENGLISH,

BY THE

REV. H. G. KEENE,

LATE ARABIC AND PERSIAN PROFESSOR, AT THE EAST INDIA COLLEGE, HAILEYBURY, HERTS.

1835.

TO THE

STUDENTS AT THE EAST INDIA COLLEGE.

GENTLEMEN,

I HAD the satisfaction for several years to serve as a Professor in your College: I wish I could think that my usefulness was equal to my earnest desire for the prosperity of our Indian Possessions; the welfare of the Natives; and the health and happiness of those who are called by Providence to the important duty of governing those ancient and interesting Nations.

At the request of the Students, I translated a portion of the ANVĀRI SUHELĪ, to help them in learning Persian.

Permit me thus to offer it to your use; partly that I may make this public avowal of the deep interest I shall always feel in the prosperity of the College; and partly that I may indulge the hope of not being forgotten among you.

I have the honour to be,

GENTLEMEN,

In great truth,

Your earnest well-wisher,

H. G. KEENE.

PREFACE.

THE sole object of this Translation is to help those who are learning Persian, to read the original with such ease, that they shall at once feel the appropriate sense of each word; and shall, imperceptibly, fall into the proper order of arranging the words, and acquire a familiarity with the idiomatic turns of the language. The learner must, however, take the trouble of referring to the Dictionary, for those words of which he does not know the original, as well as the figurative, meaning; and he must be careful to note down every example, where the grammatical construction of Persian differs from that of the Classical Languages: and then he will not find much difficulty in turning such a Translation as this back into Persian.

With these objects in view, the Translation has been made as literal as possible; and except where the passage was very simple, an attempt has been made to represent each separate word of the original, and to place the words, or at least the clauses of each sentence, very nearly in the order in which they would stand in Persian. And the consequence has been, that the language of the Translation is neither pure nor elegant; and may, in some parts, perhaps, be found incorrect and obscure.

If the object had been to amuse the reader with the story, or with an example of the ornaments of Persian composition, a very different course must have been pursued; and such faults would deserve censure: but, when the purpose is rather to teach the language, than to give the sense of the author, such defects are inevitable; and are hardly to be reckoned as such.

Those for whose service this Translation has been made, will feel both the difficulty and the usefulness of the task; and will be slow to censure those blemishes by which they benefit: if it should chance to fall into the hands of others, they are requested, in candour, to consider the object that was in view.

It would be a bold thing to say, that, even as a literal translation, it has no faults. It requires a more thorough knowledge, than any foreigner can hope to acquire, to seize the exact meaning of all those idioms, refined similies, and distant allusions, in which the Persian language abounds. And the Translator is aware, that he may have fallen into some mistakes, either from ignorance or inadvertence; and he regrets that he had not the advantage of consulting one who was able to set him right. It is hoped, however, that such mistakes, are not numerous, and that they will be viewed with indulgence.

CHAPTER I.

On avoiding the Words of a Traducer and a Talebearer.

THE great Prince Dābashalīm said to the sage Pilpai thus—the purport of the first testament was this, that when any one becomes eminent by the honor of a near intercourse with princes, he will assuredly be an object of envy to his contemporaries; and envious men labouring for the destruction of the stability of his dignity will change the mind of the king by words mingling deceit. It behoves a king, therefore, that he should reflect well upon the language of a man of selfish views; and when it is known that it is not devoid of mixture and pollution, he should not allow it to approach the confines of consent. *Couplets.* "Admit not a man of selfish designs to your presence: for he has mixed together the sweet draught, and the sting: in appearance he gives the draught, and shews kindness: in reality he strikes the sting, and works mischief." Now I entreat of the Brahman that he would relate some tale adapted to the case; and that he would set forth in detail the story of some one who may have been taken into close intimacy with a king; but by the designing language of the envious, the foundation of his station has suffered injury, and friendship has concluded in enmity, and concord in contention. The Brahman replied thus—the axis of the foundations of sovereignty are on this testament; for if a king does not restrain designing people from making strife and doing mischief, they will render the greater part of the pillars of the state vexed and mortified; and general confusion will thereby both find a way through the kingdom, and also infect the prince: and whenever a wicked promoter of strife finds room for interference between two friends, the conclusion of their business will certainly draw towards dismay and melancholy; as it was between the lion and the ox. The prince asked how that had happened.

Story.

The Brahman said. They have related that there was a certain merchant; he had measured the stations of land and sea; he had (folded) travelled over the climes of east and west; experienced the cold and heat of time; and often tasted the bitter and the sweet of the days. *Distich.*—" A prudent man, faithful and skilled in business; and by reason of experience very well informed." When the advanced guard of the army of death, which is used as a term for the debility of old age, began to rush upon the empire of his constitution; and the scouts of the army of fate, which is an allusion to white hair, took possession of the neighbouring country of the fortress of his frame. *Poetry.*—" When the drum of sickness beats the change of the watch for old age; the heart becomes cold to pleasure and enjoyment; white hair brings a message from fate; the bent back brings a salutation from death." The good man perceived that they were going each moment to beat out the drum of departure; and were about to claim back the capital stock of life, which is a store, laid up as a deposit in the house of the body; he called his children together, who were three honest and intelligent young men; but in the infatuation of riches and the impetuosity of youth, having wandered from the path of rectitude, they used to put forth the hand of extravagance on the wealth of their father; and having shewn an aversion to any trade or profession, they passed their valuable time in vanity and sloth. The affectionate father, from that excess of love and tenderness which belongs to the paternal character, began to advise his children, and opened unto them the gates of disinterested admonitions founded upon the comprehensive principles of hope and fear; and spake thus: O young men, if you do not know the value of that wealth, in the attainment of which not a single care has reached you, you are excused according to the principles of prudence; but one should understand that wealth may become a fund of happiness in this world and the next; and all that men seek of the distinctions of either world, may be obtained by means of wealth; for the people of the world are seeking for one of three conditions: the first is, abundance of living, and ease in the means of it; and this is the object of those whose wishes are founded upon drinking, and dressing, and labouring for the gratification of the pleasures of sense: the second is exaltation of rank, and increase of dignity; and that class whose object is this, they are people of distinction and eminence; and to these two conditions, it is not possible to reach except by wealth: the third is, the attainment of the rewards of futurity, and arriving at the heights of glory; and the class who turn their attention to this object are people of sanctity and holiness: and the attainment of this rank is also to be brought about by lawful wealth. The blessing of wealth is pure to a man who is pure. As the mystic sage has said in his verses. "If thou bearest wealth for the sake of religion—the prophet has said of it: good is the wealth that is pure." Thus it is plain, that by the blessing of wealth most of our objects may be accomplished; and the attainment of wealth without labour and pursuit seems impossible; and if in a few instances a man obtains wealth without trouble, since he has suffered no vexation in the attainment of it, then assuredly, not knowing the worth and value of it, he will soon fling it away; therefore departing from sloth, turn to industry, and be occupied in this art of commerce which you have so long observed in me. The elder son said :—my father, you direct us to exertion, but this is a denial of resignation ; and I know to a certainty that whatever fortune is decreed, though I should make no exertion in the pursuit of it, will certainly befal me, and that which is no part of my fortune whatever pains I may take in pursuit of it will do no good. *Verses.*—"Whatever is my lot will come in time—and that, which is not, will doubtless never happen —then, in search of that which will not come to pass— why should one suffer useless trouble." And I have heard that an eminent person has said : "Whatever was my lot, though I fled from it, it hung upon me ; and that which was not my destiny, though I clung to it, escaped me," and so whether we work or do nothing, in all respects—it is impossible to cast off from oneself the destiny of fate : as for instance, the story of those two sons of a king is an evidence of the case ; where the father's wealth fell into the hands of one without any trouble, while the other lost country and kingdom in the hope of that treasure. The father asked how that had come to pass—The son said,

Story.

In the country of Aleppo there was a king, prosperous, powerful and high in dignity; who had seen many vicissitudes of fortune, and witnessed many changes of night and day ; and he had two sons who had fallen into the whirlpool of the pride of youth, and were intoxicated with the spirit of the wine of pleasure ; and were continually given to sports and amusements, and occupied in music and festivity ; while they listened to the notes of this song from the tongue of the lute and the pipe —strive after pleasure ; for before you can shut your eye, the autumn comes on, and the fresh spring passes away. The king was wise, and a man of experience, who possessed abundant jewels and endless gold—when he saw the manners of his children, he was afraid that after him, casting all those savings into the danger of extravagance, they would give them to the wind of destruction according to their wants. Now there was a devotee in that neighbourhood, who had turned his back on worldly affairs, and set his face upon preparing the stores of futurity—he was inflamed with the beams of the manifestation of glory —bewildered in the presence of his Lord. The king had an affection for him, and had the utmost confidence with respect to him; having collected the whole of his riches, he buried them in his cell, in such a way that no one got information of it. He then gave this injunction to the holy man. "When faithless fortune and inconstant prosperity shall turn away their faces from my children; and the fountain head of prosperity, which like the mirage is nothing but an illusion, has been choked up with the dust of misfortune; and my children are reduced in circumstances and destitute; you may tell them of this treasure: perhaps, after having seen trouble and suffered difficulty, they may take warning, and may spend it in a prudent manner; and having turned from profusion and extravagance, may observe the limits of rectitude." The hermit accepted this trust from the king; and the king with a view to the expediency of the case, having prepared a well in a palace that he had, pretended that he kept his treasure buried there; and acquainted his sons, that when any occasion of necessity should arise, there was an ample treasure stored up there, upon which they might live. After this transaction, in a very little time the king and the hermit, having both obeyed the call of the Lord, fell senseless with the cup of "every soul must taste of death." Every one that is born, of necessity, it belongs to him to drink, from the cup of fate, the wine of "all creatures on the earth decay." And the treasure that was buried in the hermit's cell, remaining hidden and concealed, no one happened to get intimation of it.

After the death of the father, the brothers fell to quarrelling and fighting about the division of his dominions and wealth; and the elder, by superior strength and consequence having succeeded, took every thing into his own disposal, and left his younger brother sorrowful and forlorn. The disconsolate man, bereaved of royal dignity, and stripped of his hereditary fortune, considered with himself thus: since the sun of prosperity and pomp has turned to the west of decline, and the cruel heavens have displayed infidelity and imposture, what good can it do to set out once more in pursuit of the world, or again to make trial of what has once been tried. *Verses.*—"The whole of the world, from first to last, since it passes away, is not worth a barley-corn: betake yourself to some better kingdom than this; open the door to some pleasanter chamber than this." Nothing can be better than this, that since the collar of fortune has dropped from the grasp of controul, I will catch hold of the skirt of resignation and contentment; nor will I fling away the dignity of that holy poverty which is a royalty that never fades. The dervise to whom the treasures of contentment are consigned, has the name of dervise (a poor man); but he is the sovereign of the world. So, with this determination, he left the city, and said to himself, there was a hermit, a great friend of my father's; the wisest thing, in my condition, is to seek his cell, and at his feet, by a course of austerity follow the path of devotion. When he reached the cell he discovered that the parrot of his noble soul had taken flight from the cage of his body towards the gardens in paradise on high; and that the cell was empty of that sage of enlightened mind. For a little while, grief and sorrow at this event overcame him; at last, being satisfied with the same hermitage for his dwelling, in the warmth of his attachment he became the keeper of the place. Now there was a channel in the neighbourhood of the hermitage; and they had dug a well inside the hermitage and had made a way to the channel; so the water always came by that channel into the well, and the inhabitants of the hermitage made use of it for their total and partial ablutions. The prince let his bucket down into the well one day; but there was no sound of water; he examined narrowly and there was no water at the bottom: he began to wonder what accident had happened that the water did not come into the well; and thought if any complete obstruction had taken place in the well and the channel, and that it was altogether shut up, it would be impossible to remain any longer in the place. So in order to investigate the matter, he went down into the well, and examined every side and part of the well, and the water, and the passage with a look of minuteness. On a sudden, an excavation appeared, from which some mass had fallen into the water-course, and prevented the water from running into the well. He said to himself, why where can this excavation go to; and where can this opening end? So he made the opening a little wider; and no sooner stepped into it, than he came upon the midst of his father's treasures. The prince, as he beheld those countless riches, and that boundless wealth, prostrated himself in gratitude to God, and said, although it is immense wealth and jewels without number, yet must I not deviate from the path of resignation, nor from the way of contentment; and I must use it in proportion to my wants—that we may see what will come forth from hidden things.

On the other hand, the elder brother being established in his government, would take no care of his people and his troops; but wasted every thing that he could lay his hands upon, in expectation of the fancied treasure which he supposed to be in his father's palace; and from excess of pride and arrogance made no inquiry after his brother, but rather felt ashamed of attachment to him. When he least expected, an enemy appeared against him, and attacked his dominions with a desolating and cruel army. The prince found his treasury empty, and his troops unprovided and in a miserable state; so he came to the spot where the father had pointed out the treasure, that he might, with those great riches equip the army—no kingdom without men, and no men without money:—but the more he increased his exertions the less could he find any traces of the treasure; and the more labour and perseverance he shewed, the more was he disappointed of the attainment of his object. *Distich.*—" Listen to this secret, that you may relieve yourself from care; you will drink your blood, if you look for the provision that is not laid up for you." And when he despaired altogether of the treasure, he laid hold of all sorts of devices, and got his army in order, and, marching to repel the enemy, left the city. After the line of battle had been drawn up on both sides, and the fire of slaughter had been kindled, an arrow from the ranks of the enemy hit a vital part of the prince, and he died on the spot; on this side also they shot an arrow, and the foreign king was likewise slain; and both armies were left in confusion and without a leader. It was very near, that the fire of strife should begin to blaze, and the inhabitants of both countries be burnt in riot and disorder. At last the chiefs of both armies met together, and by mutual consultation looked out for a king of a generous nature and virtuous disposition, and for a legal house and sovereign race; to whom they might commit the business of government and the affairs of state; and the general opinion became fixed on this, that the auspicious prince whose fortunate forehead was worthy of the crown of eminence, and whose happy finger was fit for the seal of empire, was that contented prince. The men of authority of the two countries went to the door of the hermitage, and conducted the prince with the greatest veneration and honour from the corner of neglect to the court of applause; from the cell of retirement to the chief place on the throne of prosperity. Thus by the blessing of resignation, he both found the treasures of his father; and the dominions of his father were also confirmed to him. Now I have brought forward this example that it may be known for a truth, that the obtaining of what is destined for us, has no connection with labour and industry, and that to place our confidence in resignation is better than to rest upon diligence. *Verses.*—"There is no course of industry better than resignation ; what is more desirable than resigning oneself. Lo ! be resigned, and stir not hand nor foot; for thy destiny is more attached to thee than thou art to thyself. If thou hadst had a little patience, thy destined portion would have come; and flung itself upon thee like a lover."

When the son had brought this story to an end, the father said, all thou hast said is right and true; but this world is a world of means and secondary causes ; and the divine ways so proceed that the appearance of most worldly events is connected with secondary causes. And the advantages of industry are more than those of resignation; for the profit of resignation just rests with him who is resigned, and that is all; while the benefits of industry pass from the industrious man to another; and to convey benefit is a proof of virtue; for "the best of "men is he who benefits mankind;" and a man who is able to cause good to another, it would be a shame that he should take to indolence and receive benefits from others. Perhaps thou hast never heard the story of that person, who, after he had observed the fortune of the crow and the raven, laid aside industry, and by that means the divine wrath fell upon him. The son enquired how that had happened; and the father said,

STORY.

They have related, that a poor man was going through a wilderness, and meditating upon signs of mercy and instances of power: on a sudden he saw a sharp-winged falcon, having a piece of flesh in her talons, who was hovering about a tree, and going round a nest in extreme agitation. The man, wondering at the meaning of this, stopped some time to look. He saw an unfledged raven lying in the nest; and the falcon kept dividing the meat into pieces, and in proportion to the craw of the unfledged raven, put it into his mouth. The man exclaimed, "Glory to God! behold his sovereign bounty and unlimited kindness; for he doth not leave without food, in the corner of this nest, the unfledged raven, which has neither power to fly nor vigour to attack." *Verses.*—"The surface of the earth is His universal board; at this open table, what if it be foe, what if it be friend. He hath spread so wide the table of His bounty, that the Sīmurgh eats his daily bread in the mountain of Kāf." Then I, who never rest in the search of food, and who turning my head to the deserts of avarice, earn a little bread by any device; certainly this is a languor of confidence, a weakness of faith. *Verses.*—"He who sends the food is surety for the food; how long shall I run on every side, like the base: with a cheerful heart, let me fetch my breath; for whatever befals me is my lot, and no more." It is better that henceforth I should lay the head of tranquillity on the knee of retirement; and draw a line of suppression across the page of industry and business. "Our daily sustenance is with God; He is blessed and high." Then, having washed his hands of all worldly means, he sat down in a corner; and fixed his simple mind on the faultless bounty of the great first cause. "Fix not thy heart on secondary causes; and do not abandon the causer of those causes." For three days and nights he remained in a cell; but no relief appeared from any passing event; and every moment he became more weak and languid. At last debility came to excess, and the recluse became greatly reduced; and was prevented from performing the duties of obedience and prayer. The Almighty sent the prophet of that age to him, and in great displeasure gave this message, "My servant, I have laid the course of the world upon second causes, and intermediate means: and though my power is able to bring great events to pass, without any intermediate cause, yet my wisdom has ordained that the greater part of important affairs shall be prepared and accomplished by secondary means: and by this means the rule of giving and receiving benefit is extended. And thus, if thou canst be a means of advantage to another, it is better than that thou shouldst receive benefit by the means of another." *Couplet.*—"Be like the falcon; that thou mayest take thy prey, and give a mouthful: be not a base uninvited guest, like the unfledged raven." Now I have introduced the story for this, that thou mayest know that it is not practicable for all persons to reject the interposition of secondary means; and that a right resignation is, that, with attention to secondary causes, a man should be firm in his trust in God; so that he may partake of the gracious promise, "an industrious man is the friend of God." And one of our great men has said "follow some business, that thou be not slothful; yet hold thy food to be from God, that thou become not an infidel." *Verses.*—"Be not, by resignation, slothful of the means; and hear this saying, he that labours is the friend of God. If thou dost trust in God, do it in thy labours, and follow thy calling; then rely on the Almighty."

Another son then began to say, father, we have not the strength for an entire trust in God; there is no remedy against some course of exertion: but when we engage in business, and God supplies us with some wealth and provision out of the stores of his goodness, what must we do with it? The father replied, to collect wealth is easy; but to take care of it, and make a good use of it, is difficult. When money comes into the hands of any one, he must look upon two things as belonging to it. One is, that he must take care of it, in such a way that it may be safe from waste and plunder; and that the hand of the housebreaker, the highwayman, or the pick-pocket, may come short of it; for gold has many friends, and the rich man has numerous enemies. *Couplet.*—"The heavens never attack the destitute; but assault the cavalcade of the pompous." The other is, that he should derive benefit from the profits of, but not squander the capital; for if men spend all out of their stock, and are not content with the profits of it; in a very little time the dust of decay will arise out of it. *Verses.*—"Every sea to which no water runs; will soon become a dry place. If thou take from a hill, and lay nothing instead; in the end the hill will tumble down."

Whoever has no income, yet always spends; or whose expences are beyond his income; in the end he will fall into a labyrinth of poverty. It is very possible that his conduct may end in destruction; just as that wasteful rat killed himself with vexation. The son asked how that had come to pass; and the father said,

Story.

They have related that a villager had laid up a quantity of grain in store, in a barn; and had shut up every channel to the employment of it; that on the day when want should come to excess, and necessity to its limit, he might derive advantage from it. By chance a rat, who from excess of greediness would have wanted to steal grains from the granary of the moon, or to snatch with the claws of avarice, the bunch of the Pleiades from the cornfield of the sky, had a house in the vicinity of that place, and a nest in the neighbourhood of that barn. He was always digging about under ground on every side, and with his rock-rending teeth cutting a hole in every direction; on a sudden the end of the hole came out into the midst of the grain; and grains of wheat, like glittering sparks from heaven, came pouring down through the roof of his house. The rat saw that the promise of "in the heavens is your food" had come to fulfilment; and that the saying "seek your food in the bowels of the earth" was become clear. On the appearance of this abundance he poured forth the duties of thanksgiving; and, by the attainment of these jewels of great price, having got great opulence, he began to shew the pride of Crœsus, and the arrogance of Pharoah. In a little while, all the rats of the district, having got news of the particulars of the case, girded up the loins of service in attendance upon him. *Couplet.*—"These false friends, which thou seest, are flies about some sweetmeat."—These friends of the dish, and companions of the cup, collected about him: and, as their fashion is, having formed their plans of flattery, never would say a word but according to the wish of his mind, and the desire of his nature; nor ever loosened their tongues, but in praise and admiration of him. And he also, loosening his tongue in vanity and boasting, and opening his hand in prodigality, in the belief that the grain of that house would never have an end, and that wheat would always be pouring and running from that hole, used every day to expend a large quantity of it on his companions; and paying no regard to the future, never turned himself from the fancy of to-day to reflection on to-morrow. "Cup-bearer, let us drink our wine to-day, for who has ever seen to-morrow."

Now while the rats were engaged in festivity in that snug retreat, the assault of famine and a scanty year had cast down the people; and the fire of hunger was kindled in the breasts of the portionless whose hearts were consumed. On every side they would offer an object of affection for a loaf, and no one paid the least regard; in every direction they were selling the goods of their houses for a dinner, but nobody would buy them. *Verses.*—"Whoever had a desire to see a cake; might look at the orb of the sun in the heavens, and no more. By the scarcity a multitude were distressed; the hungry were lamenting, and the full hard-hearted."

The infatuated rat, having spread the carpet of indulgence and luxury, neither knew of the famine, nor was acquainted with the badness of the season. Some days went by; matters came to extremity with the peasant, and the knife was come to the bone: he opened the door of the house; and saw that a great diminution had found its way to the corn. He drew a cold sigh from his hot heart, and having suffered much regret for the loss of it, said to himself, to lament over an event, the remedy for which is beyond the bounds of possibility, is not the way of wisdom: at present it seems best to collect the rest of the corn that is in this house, and remove it to another place. So the peasant set to work in taking out the portion that was left.

Upon this occasion, the rat, who thought himself the master of the house, and the lord of the dwelling, was asleep; and the other rats, in the excess of their covetousness and greediness, never heard the sound of the peasant's feet, nor the noise of moving about over head; but one among them, quick in sagacity, being aware of the matter, got upon the roof to find out the truth of it, and observed the particulars of the case through a window; coming instantly down, and having told his friends the meaning of what was going on, he flung himself out of the hole; and they too, every one, went out to some corner; and left their benefactor alone. *Verses.*—"All are your friends for the sake of the parings; in quest of a mouthful, they have an affection for you. When your wealth falls off, they fall off in love; they would wish your ruin for the sake of their own profit. With this handful of hypocritical friends, to cut is better than friendship."

Next day when the rat raised his head from the pillow of repose, though he looked carefully to the left and right, he saw none of his friends; and the greater search he made before and behind, the fewer traces did he find of his associates. He began to exclaim and said, *Couplet.*—"The friends that were here; what is become of them: Ah! what was the matter; that they have departed from us?" So, in order to learn the truth of their proceedings, he came out of his quiet lodging, after the long period in which he had sought retirement; and having got intelligence of the calamity of the dearth, and the misery of the scarcity and high prices, he set off again in great consternation for his own house, that he might practise the utmost diligence in the preservation of the store that he had got. When he got home, he saw no traces of the wheat: and having gone by the hole into the granary there was not so much food to be found as would do for provision for one night. His endurance being bent down, he began to rend the collar of his condition with the hand of tribulation; and beat his silly head so often on the ground, that his brains were scattered: thus, by shameful profusion, he fell into the labyrinth of ruin and worthlessness.

Now the moral of the tale is this, that the expenses of a man ought to be suitable to his income; that whatever funds he may possess, he should enjoy the profits only; and should preserve his capital in such a way that no injury may happen to it. *Couplet.*—" Look every instant to your income and expenses; and when you have no income, spend the more slowly."

When the father had got through the end of his story, the younger son arose, and having arrayed the preface of his discourse with prayers and good wishes for his father, he said, but father, when a man, according to rule, has put his money by safely, and has derived a full profit from it, how is he to spend that profit. The father replied, in all things, the path of moderation is to be praised; and especially in the manner of living. The man of wealth therefore, after he has made his profits, should observe two other rules; first, he should avoid extravagance, and all unreasonable expenses, that it may not bring forth shame, and that men may not let loose the tongue of censure on him: for in truth the waste of property and extravagance in expenditure is one of the delusions of the devil. " Truly the extravagant are the brothers of devils." *Verses.*—" It is the opinion of men of great worth; that parsimony is preferable to extravagance. Though to give is on all occasions captivating; yet whatever is done in order is agreeable." Secondly, he should avoid the character of avarice, and the disgrace of parsimony: for a miser has a bad name in religion and in the world; and a worldly avaricious man is at all times reviled and the enemy of joy; and the riches of the miser become, in the end, the target of the arrow of dissipation and waste; as, for example, a large reservoir, into which water is continually flowing from several streams, and which has no outlet in proportion to the influx, it will certainly seek a way on every side, and burst out at every corner, and cracks will be made in the wall; till at last, it comes to this, that all at once being broken down and destroyed, the whole of the water is spread abroad on all sides. " Threaten the miser with misfortune, or with an heir." *Fragment.*—"That wealth from which the miser took no share; the hand of plunder scattered to the wind; or it hath fallen to some heir, who never mentions his name but to express his scorn."

When the sons had heard the advice of their father, and had clearly perceived the benefits of his discourse, each chose some occupation, and applied his hand to business. The elder brother turned himself to trade; and undertook a distant journey. He had two baggage bullocks with him: the bull of the sphere would not have had the power to contend with their strength; and the lion of the heavens, at their rage and fierceness, would, like a cat keeping a fast, conceal the claws of terror in the paw of helplessness. *Couplet*—" In stature like an elephant, in attack like a lion; haughty in look, and resolute in pace."

One was called Shatrabah, and the other Mandabah. The worthy merchant used always to provide for them, and would himself do all that was necessary for them. But as the time of the journey grew long, and they went through tedious roads, languor crept upon their condition, and traces of debility were apparent on the forehead of their state. By chance, in the course of the road, a large morass lay before them. Shatrabah stuck in it; the master gave orders, and by great stratagem they got him out: but as he had no power to move, his master hired a person whom he appointed to take care of him; and it was settled that when he should recover a little strength he would bring him to the caravan. The hired servant, having passed a day or two in the midst of the desert, was melancholy from loneliness; so having abandoned Shatrabah, he brought word to the merchant of his death. And at that stage, Mandabah, from excess of fatigue and separation from Shatrabah, ended his life. While Shatrabah, in a short period, having recovered strength enough to move, was searching about for pasture in every direction; till he came to a meadow adorned with every kind of sweet smelling plants, and arrayed in every variety of herbage, paradise, out of envy of that garden, had bitten the finger of jealousy; and the sky, at the sight of it, had opened the eye of amazement. *Couplet.*—"With flowers and fresh grass and running water; may the evil eye be far off, thou wouldst say it is another paradise."

The place was delightful to Shatrabah, and he unloaded the furniture of residence in the courts of that meadow. And when for a certain space he had grazed in that meadow, without any bond of constraint, or check of controul; and had passed the time, after the desires of his heart, in that exhilirating air and charming plain, he became extremely strong in body, and fat. The enjoyment of being refreshed, the relish of repose carried him so far that in tumultuous pleasure he bellowed aloud. There was, in the neighbourhood of the meadow, a lion of great fierceness and boldness: many of the gentle animals had bound up their loins in his service, and countless savage beasts had laid the head of obedience on the line of his authority. The lion, in the pride of youth, and the insolence of power and enjoyment, abundance of servants, and multitude of attendants, could not imagine any body greater than himself, and cared not for the tiger, quick in attack, nor the elephant, huge in shape; but he had never seen an ox, nor heard its voice; so when the bellowing of Shatrabah reached him, he was excessively frightened; and from anxiety that the wild beasts should not know that terror had come over him, he would not stir in any direction, but kept quiet in his place.

Now among his attendants there were two cunning jackals; one Kalīlah by name, the other Damanah. They both had a great reputation for intellect and sagacity; but Damanah was of greater genius, and more ambitious in the pursuit of rank and honour. Damanah by his penetration, found out in the lion that dismay had overcome him, and that he was occupied with something passing through his mind; so he said to Kalīlah, what do you say about the state of the lion; who has laid aside the pleasure of exercise, and lies still in one place. *Couplet.* —"The marks of melancholy on his forehead, have given notice of his mournful heart." Kalīlah replied, what business have you with this question? and what concern have you in saying such things? *Hemistich.*—"Whence art thou; and whence the talking of the secrets of state?" Whilst we receive our food at the court of this prince; and pass our days in repose, under the shade of his fortune, keep to this exactly; and pass on from searching into the secrets of princes, and investigating their concerns: for we are not of that set, that we can be honoured with the familiarity of rulers, or that there should be any time for attention to our opinion among kings; and therefore to talk about them is to undertake what does not belong to us: and he that undertakes to meddle in an affair for which he is not fit, the same will befal him which happened to the monkey. Damanah asked how that fell out.

STORY.

Kalīlah said, they have related that a monkey saw a carpenter seated on a piece of wood, and sawing it. He had two wedges; one he drove down into the cleft of the wood, that the sawing might be easy, and the way be open for the passage of the saw; and as soon as the cleft used to go beyond a certain limit, he would knock in the other and take out the former wedge: and in this manner he went on with his work; and the monkey kept admiring it. On a sudden the carpenter rose up, in the midst of his work, on some urgent occasion; and the monkey, the moment he saw the coast clear, sat down on the plank, and his hinder parts fell into the cleft on the side where it was sawed: he then pulled out the wedge from the cleft, which was in the front of the work, before driving in the other; and, as soon as the wedge was drawn out, the two divisions of the wood uniting together, the hind legs of the monkey were left fast in the middle of the wood. The wretched monkey, sick with pain, kept screaming and saying, *Couplet.*—"It is better that each person in the world should do his own work; for that person who does not mind his own business, will do completely wrong. My work is to pick fruit; not to use a saw: my business is to sport in the woods; not to chop with hatchet and cleaver." *Hemistich.*—"To him who does such things, thus it will happen." The monkey was in this talk with himself, when the carpenter returned and handled him as he deserved; and the monkey's work, by this addition, ended in destruction: and hence they say, *Hemistich.*—"Carpenter's work is not the business of a monkey." And I have produced this example that you may perceive that it behoves every person to follow his own business, and not to step beyond bounds: for every business there are men. And how beautifully have they said, *Couplet.*—" I remember a proverb of one of my friends, there is work for every man, and a man for every work." This is no business of your's ; let it alone ; and reckon the small portion of food and subsistence which comes to us, as great spoils.

Damanah said, whoever seeks to be about the persons of princes, ought not to do it for food and provision ; for the belly may be filled any where, and with any thing : but the advantage of paying court to kings is rather the obtaining a distinguished station that a man may in that situation be able to indulge his friends by his favour, and settle the affairs of his enemies with severity. He, whose spirit can bend the head for food, belongs to the class of animals ; like a hungry dog who delights in a bone ; or like a cat of base character, who is pleased with a morsel of bread. And I have observed that a lion, if he is pursuing a hare, as soon as he spies an ass of the desert, he will let him alone and turn to the chase of the ass. *Couplet.*—" Exalt thy spirit, for with God and man ; thy consideration will be according to thy spirit." He who gains a lofty station, though like the rose he may be short-lived ; yet the wise reckon him as living long, because of his fair fame : while he who descends to meanness and baseness of spirit, though, like the leaves of the pine, he may long continue, yet he finds no consideration with persons of eminence, and they take no account of him. *Couplet.*—" Saadi! the man of good reputation never dies: a dead man, is one whom they never speak of for good."

Kalīlah replied, the pursuit of rank and office seems good in that class, who by nobility of connections, accomplishment of manners, and high birth, have some fitness and pretension to them : but we are not of that stamp that we are adapted to high stations, or that we should make any exertion in pursuit of them. *Couplet.*—" I am dreaming about the bosom of the ocean ; alas ! what things are in the head of this drop, planning impossibilities."

Damanah said, the source of greatness is, talents and manners; not descent and connections: whoever has a clear understanding, and perfect discretion, will raise himself from the meanest station to the most honourable condition: and he who has a weak judgment, and a feeble understanding, will throw himself down from the highest station to the lowest rank. *Fragment.*—"By the service of a fine understanding and correct judgment; a man may throw the noose of disposal over the heavens; and if the eyes of the mind are not opened by high enterprise; the attention can never be turned to lofty objects." And the ancients have observed that advancement to honourable posts comes to pass by much trouble; but descent from a station of dignity is brought about with very little pains: just as one can with great fatigue raise a heavy stone from the earth upon one's back; but can throw it upon the earth by a slight movement. And it is for this reason that none, but a man of lofty spirit who is able to endure difficulties, can find pleasure in striving after high things. *Couplet.*—"To venture upon love does not become the delicate; my soul; heroes, enduring calamity, rush into this tumult." He who looks for the comfort of "obscurity is ease," having washed his hands of reputation, will be for ever a recluse in the cell of misery and disappointment: while he who never thinks of the thorny plains of "notoriety is a misfortune," in a short time, having plucked the rose of desire, he will sit down in the garden of honour on the throne of enjoyment. *Verses.*—"While he suffers not sorrow nor pain, the worth of a man does not increase; till the ruby has turned its heart into blood, it has acquired no value: the wayfaring man, in the book of his happiness; never found the writing of prosperity, without the blots of trouble."

You have perhaps never heard the story of those two fellow-travellers; one of whom by the endurance of difficulty and hardship reached the pinnacle of royalty; while the other, from sluggishness and self-indulgence, remained in the depth of poverty and distress. Kalīlah asked in what manner that had been.

STORY.

Damanah said: Two fellow-travellers, one called Sālim, the other Ghānim, were going along the road; and were getting over the halts and stages, in the society of each other. Their way lay by the skirt of a mountain, whose peak might hold the dappled grey of the sky, rein and rein; and whose waist might bind the vault, whose girdle is the Zodiack, stirrup to stirrup. At the foot of the mountain was a spring of water, in clearness like the countenance of fresh-faced, rosy-cheeked damsels; and in sweetness like the words of the sugar-lipped and the sweet in speech: and in front of this spring a large bason had been dug, and all round it shady trees were entwined. *Verses*—"On one side the branches of odoriferous shrubs had sprouted; and on the other side, the trees had shot up: the hyacinth fell down at the feet of the cypress; and the violet was prostrate before the lily."

To return to the story: the two companions arrived at that delicious point, from an alarming desert; and when they saw this pleasant spot and delightful abode, there they halted for their accustomed repose; and after resting they went walking in all directions about the bason and spring; and cast their eyes about on every side. On a sudden they saw a white stone, at the edge of the bason, on that side where the water came in; and it was thus written upon it, in characters of green, such as nothing but the pen of power could inscribe on the page of wisdom; Traveller! thou hast ennobled this resting place by the honour of a halt; know that we have made a repast for our guests, after the best manner; and have arranged a table of advantage, in the handsomest way: but the condition is this, that giving up reflection, thou shalt step into this fountain; and, having no apprehension about the eddy or the depth, fling thyself, in any way that thou canst, upon the bank; then lift on thy back the lion cut out of stone, which they have set up at the foot of the mountain; and take thyself without thought or hesitation, at one run to the top of the mountain; and that thou never relax in thy labour from dread of the ravenous beasts which will meet thee, nor the fierceness of the liver-piercing thorns which will seize thee by the skirt: for when the road ends, the tree of desire will yield fruit. *Tetrastich.*—"As long as a man does not travel the road, he will not reach the halting place; whilst he does not pluck out life, he will not pass to the world of spirits: if the whole of the world were to imbibe rays of favour; one spark of light would not fall upon the slothful man."

As soon as he comprehended the purport of the writing, Ghānim turned to Sālim, saying, come along, brother; let us measure these plains of danger with the foot of intrepidity; and let us make us every possible exertion to get a knowledge of the particulars of this talisman, *Couplet.*—"Either, in success, let us place our foot on the summit of the sphere; or, like men, lay down our head for the schemes of ambition."

Sālim said, my dear friend, merely for a piece of writing, the author of which is not known, and the true nature of which is not understood, to undertake a great danger, and upon the anticipation of a fanciful benefit and imaginary advantage, to cast oneself into great peril, is a proof of ignorance: no reasonable man would take poison to a certainty, and an antidote upon supposition; nor would any prudent man agree to vexation in hard money for the sake of tranquillity upon credit. *Couplet.*—"It is not equal, in the opinion of a wise man; one moment of sorrow with a thousand years of enjoyment."

Ghānim rejoined, my affectionate companion, the love of ease is the forerunner of meanness and baseness; but to encounter perils is a signal of fortune and honour.

Fragment.—"He who sought repose and quiet, never gladdened his heart with good fortune; and he who was alarmed at the violence of the head-ache, never drank the cup of the wine of his wishes." The mind of a man lofty in enterprise, will not condescend to mere lodging and food; and until he has gained an eminent station he will never rest in the pursuit: the rose of joy is not to be gathered without the thorn of trouble; nor can the gates of the treasury of pleasure be opened except by the key of pain: now resolution having laid hold of my bridle will lead me to the top of the hill; nor shall I think about the whirlpool of difficulty nor the endurance of the burthen of hardship. *Couplet.*—"If, in the search of it, some sorrow should befall us, it is natural; but when there is a fondness for the temple, how easy are the deserts!" Sālim replied: granted, that in the hope of the spring of prosperity, one may bear with the confusion of the autumn of distress; yet still to rush into a path that has no end, to swim through an ocean which has no visible shore, appears to be far from the path of discretion. Whoever begins upon any business, it behoves him, as he has made himself acquainted with the commencement, so also to look to the conclusion; and from the first, having considered the issue, he should weigh the injury and the advantage in the balance of reason; that he may not have suffered labour in vain, nor thrown away his valuable life to the wind of destruction. *Verse.*—"Whilst thou cannot make a firm place for thy foot, do not advance in pursuit of any affair: in all the undertakings that thou comest into, first, make straight some gap for getting out of them."

Perhaps these lines may have been written as a joke, or this writing have been traced in amusement and sport; and the fountain be a whirlpool through which it is not possible to get to the edge by swimming: and if escape should be practicable, it is possible that the weight of the stone lion may be of such sort that it is not to be lifted upon the back; and if that too should come to pass, it may be that thou wilt not be able, in one run, to get to the top of the mountain: and if all these things should be done, it is not at all known, what result they may produce. I, at least, am not a companion in this transaction; and forbid you moreover from advancing in the business.

Ghānim replied: have done with these words; for I will not turn away from my resolution for the words of any man; nor will I break the engagement that I have contracted, for the suggestions of all the devils among men and genii. I know very well that thou hast not energy to bear me company; and that thou wilt never consent to join me; look on, then, for amusement; and keep giving me a little help by thy prayers and supplications. *Couplet.*—"I know thou hast not the strength to drink wine; come then, at least, to be amused with the intoxicated."

Sālim saw that he was a man of one motive only in his proceedings: so he said, I perceive, my brother, that thou art not to be kept back, by my words, and thou wilt not give up this attempt which is not fit to be made: nor have I the strength to endure witnessing this event; nor can I be amused with a matter which is neither agreeable to my nature nor acceptable to my feelings. I find my best course to be this. *Verses.*—"That I should carry forth my own baggage from this pathless wilderness." Then, laying what baggage he had on his beast, he bade farewell to his friend, and pursued his journey.

Ghānim, having washed his heart of his life, advanced to the edge of the fountain and said, *Couplet.*—"I will plunge into the boundless deep; either to sink, or to fetch up the pearl." Then firmly binding round his loins the skirt of resolution, he stepped into the fountain. *Couplet.*—"It was not a fountain; but rather an ocean which there displayed itself in the form of a fountain."

Ghānim knew that this fountain was a whirlpool of trouble; but, having a stout heart, by swimming with confidence he got to the edge in safety. And when he was come to the bank, having recovered his breath, he lifted the lion of stone on his back with all his power and might; and, putting up with a thousand difficulties and fatigues, brought himself, at one run, to the summit of the mountain. He saw a large city on the other side of the mountain, in a sweet atmosphere and on a delightful plain. *Couplet.*—"It was a city like Paradise in goodness; and like the garden of Iram in freshness of look."

Ghānim, having halted on the top of the hill, was looking upon the city, when suddenly a sound proceeded with great violence from the lion of stone; so that the mountain and the desert began to shake: and the sound having reached the city many men came forth from right and left, and setting their face towards the mountain advanced to Ghānim. Ghānim looked on with the eye of amazement, and showed astonishment at the multitude of the people; when suddenly a party of the nobles and most illustrious coming up, saluted him with prayers and praises, and having seated him, with the utmost deference, upon a travelling horse, carried him towards the city. Then, having washed his head and body with rose water and camphor, they clothed him in royal apparel, and, with great reverence and honour, resigned the reins of the sovereignty of that country into the hand of his sufficiency. Ghānim having questioned them about the particulars of this event, received an answer after this manner. That philosophers have made a talisman in the fountain which thou didst see, and have finished that lion of stone with every degree of thought and meditation, with observation of the rising of the degrees, and the aspects of the fixed stars and the planets: and at whatever time it shall occur to the mind of any gentleman that aving passed the fountain and taken up the lion he ascends to the top of the hill, no doubt this event will come to pass at that time when death shall have overtaken the king of this city. Then the lion roars, and the sound reaching the city, the people come out; and having raised that man to the sovereignty, will pass their days in repose under the shade of his justice, until the period that his time also shall come to an end. *Couplet*—"As one departs, another comes instead; they never leave the world without some master in the house." And when, by divine command, the sun of the life of the lord of this country descends below the horizon of death, the star of the grandeur of that fortunate person rises over the summit of the mountain. And lengthened ages have past that this rule has been continued according to the usage which has been related: and this day thou art the king of this city and the sovereign of this age. *Verses.*—"The kingdom is thine; command whatsoever thou wilt." So Ghānim understood that the endurance of all these difficulties had been by the dictates of fortune—fortune, when she comes for promoting success, does every thing just as is fit.

Now I have introduced this instance, for this, that thou mayest know that the draught of luxury and enjoyment is not without the sting of vexation and trouble: to whomsoever the passion for greatness shall arise, he will never be trodden down by the base; and will never be content with a low state and base condition. And I, whilst I do not attain the rank of nearness to the lion, and do not become inserted in the company of those attached to his presence, will not lay my head upon the pillow of rest, nor extend my feet on the bed of repose. Kalilah said, from whence hast thou got the key of this gate into thy grasp; and how hast thou formed the notion of entering upon this great object? Damanah said, I intend, on this occasion, when alarm and agitation have found their way to the lion, to throw myself before him: it is possible, that by the syrup of the medicine of my advice some comfort may arise to him; and by that means my place and rank may increase in his presence. Kalīlah said, how are place and advancement with the lion to happen to thee? Or, if it should be so, since thou hast never done service to princes, and dost not know the usages and manners of attendance, in a little time, all that thou shalt have gained thou wilt give from thy hand; and thou wilt not be able a second time to apply a remedy to it. Damanah said, when a man is wise and able, interference with great affairs has no mischief for him: and whoever places reliance on his talents, in every affair, that he involves himself in, as is the condition, he will acquit himself of his duty. And another thing is this; if fortune should appear, she will show the way to whatever is necessary. And in history it has come down; that the sun of the fortune of one of the market people having become exalted, he obtained the rank of sovereignty; and an impression and a report of him were spread through the world: one of the ancient kings wrote a letter to him thus. Thy trade has been that of a carpenter; and thou mayest well know carpenter's work. Of whom hast thou learnt the arrangement of government, and judgment for transacting business. He wrote in answer: He who conferred fortune upon me, omitted not any point of instruction in sovereignty. *Verses*—"When wisdom opens the volume of teaching; that comes forth from me, which is right: to whomsoever the candle is lighted by fortune; he will collect all the means of doing well."

Kalīlah said, kings do not make all men of merit distinguished by kindness; but rather give distinction by royal favour to those connected with themselves; and who by inheritance and diligence in their service have gained some approach: and since thou neither hast any hereditary claim upon the lion, nor yet any pretensions by service, it is possible that thou mayest be excluded from his favours; and it may be a cause of some calamity.

Damanah said, whoever has obtained a lofty rank, in attendance upon the king, it has been in the way of gradual advancement; and promotion has not met them, but by their own labour and perseverance, and by the effects of the encouragement of the king. Now I also desire exactly this; it is for this that I am seeking; and that I have reconciled it to myself, to bear many troubles; and to taste many unpalatable draughts. And I know that whoever attaches himself to the courts of princes must follow five things. First, he must extinguish the fire of anger with the water of gentleness. Secondly, he must beware of the suggestions of the devil of lust. Thirdly, he must not make deceitful avarice, and mischievous covetousness triumphant over reason, his guide. Fourthly, he must lay the foundation of every measure upon truth and moderation. Fifthly, whatever accidents or nice points may occur; let him meet them with kindness and good temper. For whoever is endowed with these qualities; doubtless, his wishes shall succeed in the happiest manner. Kalīlah said, I have supposed that thou art got near to the king. By what means art thou to become the object of his regard? By what merit art thou to get rank and promotion? Damanah replied, if a close intercourse with his majesty can be managed, I will pursue five qualities. First, I will serve in perfect sincerity. Secondly, I will build my ambition on obedience to him. Thirdly, I will represent all his actions and words to advantage. Fourthly, when he sets about any affair, which is allied to good policy, and in which I perceive a benefit to the kingdom; I will set it in array before his eyes and his heart: and I will bring all the benefits and advantages of it to his observation: that his delight, in the soundness of his judgment, and the correctness of his plan, may increase. Fifthly, if he should enter upon any matter, which might have a disagreeable consequence and an unpleasant conclusion, the injury of which will revert to the kingdom, I will represent the evil of it in mild language and great gentleness; and will make him aware of the harm of the consequence of it. And as soon as the king shall perceive my merits, he will distinguish me by his indulgence and favour; and will always be inclined for my society, and fond of my advice: for no talent can lie hid; and no man of merit be without a share of the effects of encouragement and support. *Verses.*—"Merit is like musk; how long shall musk lie hid? The world is suddenly filled with perfume from its odour. Go on; labour in the exercise of thy talent; for by thy virtues the surface of the earth will suddenly be filled with rumours."

Kalīlah said, thus it seems, that thy opinion is fixed on this; and thy resolution to carry on this project is confirmed. At least, be on thy guard; for attendance upon kings is a matter full dangerous; a pursuit full difficult. Philosophers have said, that on three things no one would venture, but some blockhead who had never perceived the fragrance of reason: First, the service of a prince. Secondly, to taste poison upon an uncertainty. Thirdly, to reveal his secrets to women. And the wise have compared kings to a lofty mountain: for although there may be mines of precious jewels in it, yet upon it is also the abode of tigers and snakes and other noxious things; both to ascend it is painful; and to abide upon it is difficult. They have said also, that the society of the king is to be compared with the sea; and the merchant who undertakes a voyage by sea, either acquires great gain; or gets caught in the whirlpool of destruction. *Couplet.*—"Throughout the ocean, countless riches lie; if thou wouldest have it, safety is on shore."

Damanah said, all thou hast observed, is from a motive of benevolence: for I know that a king is like a blazing fire; he who is the nearest to it, his danger is the greatest. *Couplet.*—"Keep off from the society of a king; as dry wood from a fierce fire." But yet he who is afraid of danger, will never come to the rank of greatness. *Couplet.*—"From danger there arises greatness; for the profit of *(ten forty)* 400 *per cent.* the merchant will not pack up, if he is afraid of danger." And on three things it is not possible to commence, but by loftiness of spirit. The public service of a prince: a voyage by sea: and an encounter with enemies: and I do not find myself to be mean spirited; why therefore should I be alarmed about an office under the king. *Verses.*—"Since such is the arm of my spirit; whatever I may pursue, is in my sleeve. Dost thou desire nobility and grandeur: go on labouring with all the spirit that thou hast: in short; to whatever thou mayest lay thy hand, if thy spirit be strong, thou wilt succeed."

Kalīlah said, although I am opposed to this plan, and am dissatisfied with this resolution; yet since thy judgment has so much confidence in this affair, and thy mind has such reliance on this notion; may it be fortunate: behold thy direct road; go on happily in peace.

Damanah departed; and made his obeisance to the lion. The lion asked what person that was. They said, the son of such a one, who, for a long time was an attendant upon the royal court. The lion said; true, I recollect him, so he called him forward and said, where dost thou live? Damanah replied; according to the custom of my father, I am now become an attendant at this court, resembling the firmament; and have made it the shrine of my wants, the temple of my wishes: and I wait in hopes, that, if any weighty matter should fall out, I may provide for it by my sagacity, and may enter upon it with a clear understanding. For as there is need of the pillars of the state and the chief nobles of the presence, in the fulfilment of many important affairs, it is possible that, at the courts of princes, a matter may occur, which may be accomplished by those of low degree : in this path, like the peacock, the fly also is of use : the work which is produced by a weak needle ; the spear, tossing up its head is unequal to the management of it ; and the design which an insignificant penknife executes, the sword of high temper would be at a loss in it. Nor is any servant, though he be of no estimation, and of little worth, devoid of use for removing evil, or attaining good ; since even that dry stick, which lies in contempt in the foot path, has the capacity of, some day, becoming useful ; and if it is good for nothing else, perhaps men may make a toothpick of it, or may, by means of it, clear their ears of foulness. *Couplet.*—" If a handful of flowers cannot be got from me ; I may at least serve for wood for the kettle."

The lion, when he heard the words of Damanah, being astonished at his eloquence and rhetoric, turned to his grandees, and said : though a wise man should be of no reputation, yet his understanding and knowledge will, against their will, make his talents conspicuous to the nation ; like a flame of fire, which, though he who kindles may want to make it turn downwards, will to a certainty fly upwards. *Couplet.*—" Whoever bears the stamp of true love to his mistress ; it will be manifest upon his forehead."

Damanah was delighted at these words ; and saw that his device had taken effect upon the lion, and that his deceit was completely effectual : so he loosened the tongue of advice and said : It is incumbent on the whole of the personal attendants and servants of state, that, whatever may befal the king, they should reflect upon it, according to their understanding and knowledge ; and should then represent, whatever may occur to the mind of each ; nor should they ever desert the path of good advice ; that the king may thoroughly know his followers and dependents ;

and being acquainted with the extent of the judgment, the management, the sincerity and discrimination of each, may both take advantage of the services of each, and also favour every one according to his merits; for while the seed is concealed under the curtain of the earth, no man will take the trouble to cultivate it; but when the veil of the earth is withdrawn from its face, and it raises its head in a green mantle from the collar of the ground, it may be known that it is a fruit-bearing tree, or a profitable shrub; and no doubt they will then cultivate it, and derive profit from its fruit. Yet the source, in all particular cases, is the encouragement of princes; to whomsoever, among men of talent, they may give distinction by a look of favour, from that person they will derive benefit in proportion to that encouragement. *Couplet.*—"I am like brambles and dust; thou the sun and the cloud: I may yield flowers and tulips, if thou dost give fertility."

The lion said: How ought one to cultivate clever men; and by what means can one enjoy the fruit of them? Damanah replied: The great principle in this business is this: that the king should look to worth, not birth; and if any party of incapable people should make use of the services of their fathers and ancestors, he should pay no regard to it; for a man should make good his descent by his merits, not by his father. *Verses.*—"Expand thy chest for thine own talents; do not make an ancient descent a stock of worth: O thou, insufficient, live not by one that is dead; but do thou keep thy dead alive by a good name: do not boast, young man, of a father who is no more; or else thou art a dog, when thou rejoicest in bones."

The mouse, although it be a fellow lodger with men, because of the mischief and hurt which comes from it, they think it necessary to take pains to destroy it: but the hawk, which is wild and strange, since some advantage can be anticipated from it, they allure it with the utmost kindness; and bring him up to exercise, with great kindness, on the wrist of indulgence. It therefore behoves a king, that he should not regard friends and strangers; but rather seek the wise and clever; and not allow a preponderance to those persons, who are negligent in business or destitute of talent, over men of genius and of perfect skill: for to give the post of the wise to the unwise, is the same as fixing the ornament of the head upon the feet, or to hang the apparel of the feet upon the head. And in whatever place people of talent remain lost, while men of ignorance and folly take the reins of power into their hands, the utmost confusion will find its way into the affairs of that kingdom; and the disgrace of that circumstance will attach to the fortune of the king and the people. *Couplet.*—" O noble bird, no, never cast thy glorious shade across that land where parrots are beneath the rooks."

When Damanah was done with his speech, the king, having bestowed the utmost attention upon him, made him of the number of the select nobles of his presence, and having got a partiality and affection for his conversation, he laid the foundation of all his affairs upon his counsel and advice. Damanah too, following bright reason and sagacity, understanding and penetration, in a very short time became the confidant of the secrets of government; and in promoting and improving the affairs of the kingdom and the state, he was the man relied upon, and referred to.

One day, having found the time auspicious, and the occasion favourable, he sought a private audience, and said. It is a long time that the king has remained quiet in one place; and has laid aside the pleasure of exercise, and the delight of hunting: I wish that I could tell the cause of it, and might discourse upon the point, in every form that may be in my power. The lion wished to keep the circumstance of his alarm concealed to Damanah. In that interval Shanzabah gave a fierce roar; and his voice agitated the lion so much that the reins of self-possession fell from his hands: and by force he revealed his secret to Damanah, and said: The cause of my terror, is this voice that you hear, and I do not know whose voice it may be; but I suppose his force and structure must be suitable to his voice: if such should be the fact, it is not good for us to remain here. Damanah said: Is there not, besides this voice, any other mental occupation to the king? The lion said: No. Damanah said: It is not fit for such a matter to migrate from your hereditary place, or to depart from your beloved birth-place: what respect is there for a voice; what weight to a shout; that, any one for that should move from his place? A king ought to be, like a mountain, stedfast; so as not to be shaken with every wind; nor to move from his place at every outcry. That you may not shake with every wind; draw your foot under your skirt, like a mountain. And the ancients have said that attention is not due to every loud voice, nor to every powerful body; for not every outer form gives proof of an inward meaning; nor is every external shape a pattern of the mind within: a reed, though ever so thick, may be broken by a thin stick; and a heron, though so huge in shape, is unequal to a hawk of delicate make: and whoever makes any account of a large figure, that will happen to him which befell the fox. The lion asked how that was.

STORY.

Damanah said: They have related that a fox was going through a plain; and roaming about on every side in quest of food; he came to a tree, on one side of which they had suspended a drum; and whenever a little wind used to blow, a branch of the tree would reach the top of the drum, and a shocking noise would arise from it. The fox saw a domestic fowl beneath the tree, which was digging her beak into the ground, and looking for food:

so lying in wait for her, he intended to make her his prey; when, suddenly, the sound of the drum reached his ears: he looked, and saw a figure excessively fat, and a monstrous voice was heard; the appetite of the fox being excited, he thought to himself that the flesh and the skin must certainly be in proportion to the voice; so he came out from where he was lurking for the fowl, and advanced to the tree. The fowl, being aware of the circumstance, fled; and the fox, with a hundred exertions, got up the tree; he laboured a long time till he tore the drum; but he found nothing but some skin and a bit of wood. The fire of remorse fell upon his head, and tears of shame began to pour from his eyes; and he said: Alas! that for the sake of this huge frame which was all wind, the lawful prey has escaped from my hands; and no profit has come to me from this unmeaning form. *Verses.*—"The tabor is always in lamentation, but what is the result, since there is nothing within; if thou hast any knowledge, seek for the meaning; be not deluded by the form, for that is nothing."

And I have related this story, in order that the king may not relinquish his exercise and his love of hunting for a frightful noise or a huge form; if he will observe carefully, no use can come of that voice and figure; and if the king should give orders, I can go close up to it, and will explain to the king the meaning of the case, and the real nature of the matter. The words of Damanah were agreeable to the lion; and in conformity with the directions of the lion he set out towards the sound. But as soon as he was got out of the sight of the lion, the lion reflected a little, and was ashamed of having sent him, and said to himself, I have made a gross mistake; and an act has been done by me, thoughtlessly: the ancients have said that a king in revealing his secrets should not rely upon ten classes; and should not communicate to them a hint of those private purposes in the concealment of which he takes care. First, any one who has suffered severity, and vexation at his court, without crime or offence; and the period of whose trouble and distress has lasted long. Secondly, he whose wealth and honour have gone to the winds in attendance on the king; and to whom the means of subsistence are become narrow. Thirdly, he who has been displaced from his office, and who has no hopes of again obtaining employment. Fourthly, a wicked mischievous man; who seeks after strife, and has no inclination towards security and repose. Fifthly, an offender whose friends have experienced the pleasure of forgiveness, while he has tasted the bitterness of punishment. Sixthly, a guilty man, to whose equals some slight reproof has been given; while, in his case, greater excess has been shewn. Seventhly, he who does acceptable service, and remains disappointed; while others, without any previous claims of service, meet with greater encouragement than he does. Eighthly, he, whose rank some enemy has sought after, and has taken the lead of him, and has attained to that station; and the prince has become confidential with him. Ninthly, he who anticipates any advantage to himself, in an injury to the king. Tenthly, he who has met with no favour at the court of the king; and who can make himself acceptable with the enemy of the king. It behoves kings that they should never communicate their secrets to these ten classes. And the principle is this, that till they have often tried the religion, integrity, the generosity and nobleness of any one, they should not make him master of the knowledge of their secrets. *Couplet.*—"Disclose not thy secrets to every one: for in this ball of earth we have wandered much; a safe confidant for secrets was not to be found." And therefore, in obedience to these premises, before making any experiment of Damanah, to make such haste was not suitable; and to send him to my enemy seemed very far from the course of deep thinking prudence: for this Damanah seems a shrewd person, and he has been for a long time vexed and disappointed at my court. If, God protect us ! any thorn of displeasure should be rankling in his heart, he may on this occasion contrive some perfidy, or excite some contention ; or it may be that he may find my enemy superior to me in strength and pomp; and feeling a preference for his service, he may make him acquainted with whatever he is acquainted with of my secrets ; and most certainly, to make amends, for that would be beyond the point of my management. Why did I not act up to the purport of the saying ; *Circumspection is (to have) a bad opinion :* why did I deviate from the meaning of this couplet of the philosopher. " Be not of a bad temper ; but be of a bad opinion ; and then be in safety from strife and deceit." If any calamity should be coupled with this embassy, I am deserving of a hundred times as much. In this course of thought, with great agitation, he was getting up, and sitting down ; and fixed his eyes in expectation on the road ; when all at once Damanah appeared. The lion was a little quieted ; and rested in his place. As soon as Damanah arrived, he said, after paying due homage, as long as the sphere shall revolve, may our king be permanent ; may the sun of his fortune be shining over the heads of his servants. O prince, ruling the world, he whose voice reached the august hearing is an ox, engaged in grazing in the environs of this forest ; and who has nothing else to do but to eat and to sleep ; and his ambition does not extend beyond his throat and his belly. The lion said : What is the extent of his power ? Damanah replied : I did not observe any dignity or magnificence about him, which I could take as a proof of his power : and I did not find in my own mind any awe of him, that I should reckon any great reverence due to him. The lion said you must not set him down for debility; nor be deceived by that; for a violent wind, though it does not beat down the tender grass, will tear up strong trees from the roots; and princes and nobles, as long as they do not find an enemy their match, the manifestation of their strength and importance does not come into display. When will a hawk shew any eagerness in pursuit of a chaffinch? A falcon will not open his claws to hunt a gnat.

Damanah said: The king should not give so much weight to his conduct; nor make so much account of the thought of him; for I, with great penetration, have found out his business, and am informed of the nature of his condition: if superior sense should dictate, and the august command should receive the honour of promulgation, I will bring him; that, laying the head of attention on the line of obedience, he may cast the saddle-cloth of servitude on the shoulder of attachment.

The lion was delighted at these words; and made signs for bringing him. So Damanah went up to Shanzabah, and with a stout heart, without any thought or hesitation, joined in conversation. At the first moment he said to him:—whence art thou, and how didst thou fall into this place; what was the cause of thy coming to this abode; and forming the scheme of residing here? Shanzabah began to detail the circumstances of the case, according to the truth. Damanah, having become acquainted with his history, said: A lion, who is the king of beasts, and the sovereign of these borders, has given orders, and sent me, that I should take you before him; and in like manner has given orders that, if you make haste, he will pass over the defect, which has till this moment appeared, in dutiful attention; but if you delay, I will instantly go back and set forth the form of the occurrence. Shanzabah, when he heard the name of lion and beasts, was frightened, and said: If you will make me strong hearted, and safe from his punishment, I will come with thee; and by means of thy keeping me company will have the honour of paying my duty to him.

Damanah repeated an oath to him; and brought forward such a promise and engagement, that some tranquillity might thereby grow up in his mind; and they both turned their faces towards the lion. Damanah went before and gave the lion notice of his approach; and a short time after the ox arrived, and performed the ceremony of homage. The lion addressed him with warmth and said: When didst thou come to this neighbourhood; and what was the motive for coming? The ox related his history, to the full. The lion replied: Then still remain here; that thou mayest obtain a full share of our kindness, condescension, gentleness, and bounty; for we have opened the gates of favour to the faces of all who attach themselves to our country, and have spread the overflowing table of regard before all the attendants on our threshold. *Verses*—"If through these realms you wander far; of us in lamentation you'll not find a man: at first, in any matter that we make our aim; regard unto the welfare of the lowest class we pay." The ox having set forth the prescribed form of prayer and praise, bound the girdle of service, in cheerfulness and alacrity, round his loins. And the lion, too, having bestowed on him a place of near access, brought him day by day nearer to his person; and used to shew great force and length of speech, in doing him honour and respect: in the course of which, having turned his mind to the examination of his character and the investigation of his conduct, he perceived the measure of his judgment and prudence, and the extent of his discrimination and experience; he found him to be a person famous for perfection of sagacity, and endowed with understanding and penetration; and the more he tried his moral qualities the greater became his confidence in the abundance of his knowledge. *Verses*—"He found him excellent in disposition, clear in judgment; a weigher of words, and estimating the value of men; one who had seen the world, and collected knowledge; who had travelled much and profited by society. So the lion, after meditation and counsel, deliberation and seeking for guidance, made the ox the confidant of his secrets; and every hour, his place in favour and advancement became more noble; and his rank in the exercise of authority, and the issuing of commands, more elevated; till he surpassed the whole body of the pillars of the state, and the chief nobles of the presence.

When Damanah perceived that the lion carried his reverence for the ox to the last verge of excess; and that having pushed the exaggeration of bounty and respect to him beyond the limits of moderation, he sets no importance upon *his* words, nor takes advice with him in any project—the hand of envy drew the ointment of disgust across the eye of his heart; and the fire of anger cast a blaze of jealousy into the cell of his brain. *Couplet.*—"Envy, wherever it kindles a fire—from the very first, it burns the envious themselves." Sleep and rest departed from him; tranquility and repose removed their furniture from the area of his bosom. He went with his complaint to Kalīlah, and said, My brother; behold the weakness of my judgment, and the infirmity of my contrivance: I had built all my projects upon the carelessness of the lion, and introduced the ox to his service; till having found access and dignity, he has surpassed all the courtiers; and I am fallen from my own place and station. Kalīlah replied: My life! thou hast done it thyself; what remedy is there for an act of thine own? thou hast thyself struck this axe on thine own foot; this dust of mischief thou hast thyself stirred up in thine own path: and the same thing has befallen thee, which happened to the devotee. Damanah asked how that was.

Story.

Kalīlah said. They have related that a king gave splendid apparel, and a costly dress to a devotee. A thief, having got intelligence of the circumstance, fixed his affections on it; and having, upon pretence of attachment, got about the devotee, shewed a fondness for his service: and used to evince much perseverance in acquiring the practices of the right road; till he became in this way his confidential friend; and one night, having found an opportunity, he purloined the dress and walked off. On the following day, the devotee could not find the clothes, and missed his new disciple; and knew that he had taken away the dress. He set off for the city in pursuit of him; and by the way saw that two wild beasts were fighting together, and wounding each other's heads; and while these two sharp-clawed enemies, like two destructive lions, were in conflict with each other, and the blood was trickling from the limbs and members of both, a fox had come up and was devouring their blood. On a sudden, in the midst of their butting, the fox got between them, and their heads came violently on each side against his ribs; and he was caught in the snare of destruction. The devotee having a fresh piece of experience from this event, passed on; and at night when he reached the city, the gates were locked. He wandered about in every direction, and looked for some place for a halt; by chance a woman was looking into the street from the terrace of her house; she perceived from the wandering manner of the devotee that he was a foreigner; and invited him to her own home. The devotee having agreed, untied his sandals in her lodging, and betook himself to his prayers in a corner of that hut. Now the woman was well known for vice and profligacy; and used to keep a number of girls ready for gross and dissolute behaviour; and a strong affection had grown up in one of them (a glance of whose beauty might have taught the brides of paradise the art of shining; and from the glow of her cheeks, the sun giving warmth to the earth, would have burnt in the flame of jealousy; her wanton eye, with the arrow of a glance, would have torn the target of the bosom, like the breast of a target; and her life bestowing lips, with the sweetness of her mouth, would bestow on the palate of the heart lusciousness, like a bale of sugar. *Couplet.*—"A moon, walking in majesty; a lofty cypress: two ringlets from her temples, entwined; like a noose made of musk:"—from her silver chin a ball arose, upon which a collar of double chin was suspended; with that collar and that ball, that idol, seeking love, had robbed the moon of her glory, and taken the ball from the sun,) for a youth, fair in face, musk-haired, witty in speech, a tall cypress, a silver moon, sweet in tongue, slender in the waist; so that the proud beauties of Tartary were like a hyacinth, full of writing and disorder, for the curls of his ringlets; and the honey-lipped maidens of Samarcand, in love for his strife-exciting sweetness, were like the hearts of lovers, in agitation. *Couplet.*—"A face! Oh what a face! a face like to the sun; ringlets! what ringlets! each curl was madness and distress." They constantly passed their time together, like the sun and the moon in the same mansion; and were united, like Venus and Mercury in the same sign of the Zodiac; and the youth, from the jealousy of his love, would positively never allow that his companions should drink a single draught from the goblet of union with that damsel; nor that the thirsty travellers, through the deserts of pursuit, after all their sufferings, should reach that sweet fountain. *Couplet.*—"My jealousy of thee is such, that if it were in my power; I would not allow that thou shouldest enter into bonds with others." The profligate woman, being vexed with this behaviour of the girl; and being unable to bear the loss of income; could not put up with a girl who had thrown aside the veil of modesty; and thus exposed the very life of the affection of lovers. In despair, she resolved upon the destruction of the youth; and the same night the devotee came to her house, having made her plan and watched her opportunity: and having measured out heavy draughts both to the lover and his mistress; as soon as all the people of the house were gone to rest, having put a little deadly poison, pounded, into a pipe, and placed it before the nose of the youth; taking one end of the pipe into her own mouth, and applying the other end to his nostril; she meant to give it a puff and send the effects of the poison to the brain of the young man: when all at once he sneezed; and by the violence of the vapour which burst from his brain, all the poison went down the woman's throat and gullet, and she fell dead on the spot. Even in the thought of that thou shalt go which thou bearest in mind.

The devotee, when he had witnessed this occurrence, and with a hundred anxieties, had brought to day that night, which in tediousness was like the day of resurrection; till the time that the devotee of the dawn, escaping from the cell of the darkness of the night, spread the carpet of reverence before the shrine of the horizon; and the sense of this text, high in distinction "and he will send them forth from darkness into light" was become clear to the inhabitants of the earth. *Couplet.*—"The vault, like a mirror in colour, received splendour; the mirror of China got clear of rust." The devotee having extricated himself from the abode of the darkness of the profligacy and sensuality of that gang, looked out for another lodging.

A shoemaker, who used to reckon himself among his disciples, took him to his house, as a means of obtaining a blessing; and gave injunctions to his family to take care of him: but went himself to a feast of some of his friends. Now his wife had a lover, of a cheerful temper, beautiful face, and curling locks. *Couplet.*—"Facetious, alluring, saucy-eyed and throwing glances; a handsome man, who should be like him, would be a calamity to life." The messenger between them was a barber's wife, who by her witchcraft would mix water and fire together; and by the smoothness of her tongue would make a stone quarry seem like melted wax. *Verses.*—"A contriver of stratagems, who, in deceit, would repeat some verse, which would unite the gnat with the phœnix—a crystal rosary she had for use; but for a string a pagan's thread she took: her lip in prayer, and all her prayer was magic and a trick; without plain garments; and within all paint."

The shoemaker's wife, as soon as she found the house clear, sent some one to her messenger to say, give the news to my beloved, that to night there is honey without the buzzing of the bee, and a party free from the clamour of the watchman and police. Arise and come to me; as I have learnt, and thou. So her lover coming by night to the house, was waiting for the door to be opened; when, all at once the shoemaker returned, like an unexpected calamity; and found the man at the door of his house. The fact being that he had already taken up a little fancy; and that some suspicion had fallen into his mind, about the designs of his wife, and her lover; upon this occasion, when he found him at the door of the house, the side of conviction having predominated, he entered the house, and in great anger, began to beat his wife; and when he had applied the full chastisement, he tied her fast to a pillar, and laid his head on the bed of repose. The devotee was thinking thus,—without any apparent cause, or clear offence, to beat this woman was from the course of manly feeling,—it would have been proper that I should have interceded, and not to have been consenting to this folly; when suddenly the barber's wife came in, and said, My sister; why dost thou keep this young man waiting so long; walk quickly forth, and count the season of enjoyment great gain. *Couplet.*—"If to a lover, there is a thought of asking for one sick with pain; come on joyfully for still there is a little breath in him." The shoemaker's wife called her close to her, in a melancholy voice and said. *Verses.*—"O tranquil in mind, how canst thou understand the state of an afflicted heart—how canst thou know the sufferings of lovers, of wounded hearts;

O dove, taking thy flight over the head of the cypress—how canst thou know the grief of heart of captive birds ?" My kind, kind friend ! listen to the complaint of my distress, and attend to my sad condition : this cruel merciless husband has perhaps seen him at the door ; for he came into the house like a madman, and after he had beaten me severely, tied me with great violence to this pillar : if thou hast any love towards me, and art in the place of pity to my friend, unbind me quickly, and give me leave that I may tie thee in exchange for myself to this pillar : and having quickly made an apology to my friend I will come back and unloose thee. And by this act thou wilt make me pledged to gratitude ; and thou wilt also lay my lover under obligation. The barber's wife, from excess of kindness, having yielded herself for the unloosing of the other and the tying up of herself, sent her out.

A clue to the quarrel of the husband and wife fell into the grasp of the devout man, on hearing these words. And in the meantime the shoemaker, waking, called out to his wife ; but the barber's wife, for fear he should know her voice, and get intelligence of the matter had not the power to give an answer. Though the shoemaker screamed ; not a breath was perceived from the barber's wife : so the fire of his rage bursting into a flame he took up a heel-knife and coming to the pillar cut off her nose and laid it in her hand, saying, Lo ! a present, that thou mayest send to thy lover. The barber's wife did not, from fear, utter a sigh, but said to herself, here is a wonderful state of things—one takes the pleasure ; and another bears the pain.

When the shoemaker's wife came back, and found her whom she called a sister, with her nose cut off, she was excessively distressed; and often begging pardon, she released her, and tied herself to the pillar; and the barber's wife set off home, with her nose in her hand. *Verse.*—

" In her astonishment, one moment she would laugh, and the next moment weep." The devotee had been observing and listening to all these occurrences; and surprise was added to surprise, at all the strange things which came forth from behind the curtain of secrecy.

The shoemaker's wife was quiet for a little while; and then, with cunning and deceit, spreading her hands in prayer, she said, O Lord and king! thou knowest how my husband has done me violence; and by calumny and falsehood, has bound upon my neck a crime which was never committed by me. Of thy goodness, take pity, and restore my nose, the ornament of the page of beauty. During the prayers of the woman, the man was awake; and listened to her deceitful complaint, and mischievous prayer: so he roared out. Worthless and of corrupt life! what prayer is this thou makest; what desire for thee to have! The prayers of the profligate are of no worth at this court; the desires of the vicious find no quality of fitness along this road. *Couplet.*—" If thou hast a hope that any matter should be made easy, from secret means; a pure tongue, and a pure heart are both necessary." Then the woman on a sudden shouted out, Oppressor and tormenter; get up, that thou mayest behold the divine power and infinite bounty: for since my mantle was pure from the stain of this aspersion, the Almighty has healed my mutilated nose; and has delivered me from ignominy and disgrace among mankind. The simple-hearted man arose; and when he had lighted a lamp, approached and found his wife safe, and her nose in the right place; nor could he any where find any trace of a wound or hurt. He instantly acknowledged his fault; began to make apologies; with the utmost tenderness begging pardon, removed the bonds from her hands and feet; and made a vow, that he would never proceed in a similar manner, before some clearness of proof, some manifestation of argument; that he would not vex his pious wife, his chaste spouse, upon the word of every mischief-making back-biter; and that for the rest of his life he would never depart from obedience to such a woman, veiled in virtue, and against whose prayers there was certainly no curtain.

While, on the other hand, the barber's wife, with her nose cut off, and carried in her hand, came home; but horror overwhelmed her: for, what plan could she devise; how was she to reveal this event to her husband; what excuse could she make to her friends and neighbours on this subject; what sort of answer should she give to the questions of her relations and friends. In the meanwhile the barber awaked, and called to his wife thus: Give me my instruments; for I am going to a certain gentleman's house. The woman was very long in answering; and having delayed to give him the things, at last put the razor only into the artist's hand. The barber, in a rage, flung the razor, in the darkness of night, towards his wife; and began to utter abusive words; but the woman threw herself down, and began to scream, My nose; my nose! The barber was confounded; and their friends and neighbours coming in, found the woman, with her garments stained with blood, and her nose cut off. So they let loose the tongue of reproach against the master; and he, poor fellow, being left confused, had neither the face to confess it, nor the tongue to deny.

However, when dawn, giving light to the world, cast away the veil of darkness; when the world-displaying mirror of the sun, began to sparkle like a goblet of Jamshed. *Couplet.*—" The leader of the forces of the east raised his standard; the king of the west was drowned in a sea of blood." The relations of the woman having met together, carried the barber before the Kāzī. By chance, the devotee had left the shoemaker's house; and because of an old bond of attachment which there was between him and the Kāzī, was present in the court. They fulfilled the usual form of interrogatory; and when the kinsfolk of the barber's wife presented their case, the Kāzī put this question: Master barber, how could you think fit to make an example of this female, without any apparent crime, or legal cause? The barber was astounded, and unable to set up any pretence: and the Kāzī, under this decisive text, "and wounds, retaliation:" passed sentence of retaliation and punishment.

The devotee arose and said, O Kāzī, in this matter, some deliberation must be made; and the eyes of sagacity must be opened. For the thief did not carry off my coat; the wild beasts did not kill the fox; the poison did not destroy the profligate woman; the shoemaker did not cut off the nose of the barber's wife: but rather we have drawn down all these evils upon ourselves. The Kāzī restrained his hand from the barber, and looked at the devotee, saying: Give some interpretation of this summary; some explanation of your meaning. So the devotee related all that he had heard and seen, from first to last, and said. If I had not had a desire to take a pupil, and had not been beguiled by the agreeableness of the thief, that deceitful impostor could not have found the opportunity; and would not have taken away my garment. If the fox had not gone beyond bounds in greediness and baseness, nor shown such excess in blood-thirstiness, the injury of the beasts had not reached him. If the wicked woman had not formed the design of destroying the unsuspicious youth, she had not thrown her own sweet life to the winds. And if the barber's wife had not given her assistance in that unlawful action, she had not become an example, nor been made a disgrace. He who does evil, must not look for good: and he who expects sugar canes, must not sow the seeds of the colocynth. *Couplet.*—"Thus spake a learned teacher: do not evil, or thou wilt meet with evil from fortune."

And I have produced this instance, that thou mayest know, that thou hast thyself shown this path of difficulty to thyself, and hast thyself opened this gate of sorrow and labour to thyself. *Verse.*—" After all, of whom can we complain; of ourselves is all that is upon us."

Damanah said, Thou sayest truly; I did the thing myself. And yet what scheme dost thou form for my deliverance; and in what manner dost thou view the plan for untying this knot. Kalīlah said, From the first moment I did not agree with thee in this proceeding, nor did I coincide with thy words in undertaking this business. And now also, I find myself far from the matter, nor do I see any reason for involving myself in it. Perhaps thou wilt thyself think of some plan in thy own behalf; as they have said. *Verse.*—" Every man best understands what is for his own good."

Damanah replied, I have been thinking that I will set about this business, with the finest stratagems; and will labour, by every means that may be possible, till I throw down the ox from this position; and even drive him out of the country; for I cannot permit of delay or negligence in the duty of self-preservation; and if I commit the least carelessness, I shall not be acquitted in the opinion of men of prudence and manly spirit. Nor do I seek any new advancement; nor pretend to any thing beyond my services. And our forefathers have said, that the wise are justified, when they labour for these five purposes. First, In seeking that rank and station which they may have formerly held. Second, In avoiding the hurt of that which may have come by experience. Third, In preserving that advantage which they possess. Fourth, In extricating themselves from the labyrinth of any calamity which may be impending. Fifth, In watching the attainment of good, or the averting of evil, in time to come. And I apply my exertions to this; that I may again attain to my own place; and that the lustre of my condition may be fresh: And this is the path; that I should pursue the ox with stratagems; until he bid farewell to the back of the earth; or pack up his things from this place. Nor am I less than that weak sparrow, which obtained his revenge of the falcon. Kalīlah asked how that was.

Damanah said. I have heard that two sparrows had fixed their nest upon the branch of a tree, and of all worldly possessions were content with water and grain. And at the top of the mountain, at the foot of which that tree had lighted, a hawk had his abode; who at the time of pursuing his prey would dart out from a corner like lightning, and like a thunderbolt would burn clean up the barns of life of the birds, more feeble in wing. *Couplet.*—"At the moment when he would open his talons upon the birds—if there should be fifty, he would carry them off."

Whenever the sparrows produced young, and it came near to that time, when they should take to flight, that hawk, darting out from ambuscade, having carried off their young, would make them a meal for his own young ones.

Now to migrate from that place was intolerable to the sparrows, according to "love of home is a part of faith;" and yet, because of the tyranny of the hawk, pursuing cruelly, the power of living there was difficult. *Verse.*—"Neither any view to travel, nor any mind to stay."

On one occasion, their young ones having got strength, and having put forth feathers and wings, were making a little movement; and the father and mother growing pleased at the sight of their children, were testifying joy at their exertions for flight. On a sudden, the thought of the hawk passed over their mind; and all at once, folding up the carpet of delight, in agitation and uneasiness, they began lamentation and weeping. One of their children, in whose forehead the marks of truth and maturity were apparent, enquired into the circumstances of the case, and the cause of the change from joy to sorrow. They said. O son! *Couplet.*—"Ask us not to what extent is the fire of our hearts; ask of the tear, that is our interpreter."

Then they related in detail, the story of the tyranny of the hawk, and the carrying away of their children. The son said. To turn the neck away from the command of fate and the order of destiny, is not the way of servants: yet the causer of causes has appointed a medicine for every pain: and has sent a cure for every illness: it is possible that if ye shall fulfil in the repulse of this calamity, exertion shall raise your foot in untying this knot,—both this evil shall be averted from our head, and also this burthen shall depart from off your hearts. These words were agreeable to the sparrows: so one of them waited to attend to the condition of the young, and another took flight in search of relief.

When he had flown a little way, he fell into the consideration of this, *viz.*—Ah! whither shall I go; and to whom shall I tell the anguish of my heart? *Couplet.*—"I am entangled in the pains of my heart; I know not the medicine for my heart; the remedy for the pains of the heart is a matter very difficult; I do not understand it." At last, he turned in his mind thus—Any animal, upon whom my sight may first fall, I will fix my conversation with him, and will seek from him a cure for the pain of my heart. By chance, a salamander, having come forth from the mine of fire, was taking a little turn in the open space of the desert; and the eyes of the sparrow fell upon him: and that strange figure and surprising form came into his view. He said with himself, I have fallen upon good: come on; while I communicate to this wonderful bird the grief of my heart: perhaps he may loosen the knot from my affairs; and shew me the way to relief. Then with great reverence he approached the salamander, and after the prescribed forms of good wishes, observed the usages of duty. The salamander, too, in the language of attention to strangers, set forth the duties of courtesy to travellers, and said. The traces of grief are to be observed in thy countenance; if it be from the fatigue of the road, rest a few days in this neighbourhood, that it may be changed by repose: and if any other particular case exists, explain it, that pains may be taken, to the extent of my powers, in providing for that. The sparrow loosened his tongue, and unfolded before the salamander his melancholy state in such a manner, that if he had been telling it to the marble rock, it must have split in pieces at the anguish of his heart. *Couplet.*—"To whatever person I may give an explanation of my story—I place a hundred fresh scars upon the heart of that helpless person." The fire of compassion began to blaze in the salamander, after hearing these words; and he said. Do not grieve; for I will avert this evil from thy head; and this night I will so manage, that I will burn his house and nest and all that is in it: do thou give me the marks of thine own dwelling, and go to the care of thy children, till the time that I shall come unto thee. The sparrow set forth the marks of his abode, in such a manner that no doubt could remain to the salamander: and with a joyful heart, and a mind relieved from a load of grief, set his face towards his nest. When the night came on, the salamander, with a party of the sons of his own race, each having taken up a piece of naphtha and brimstone, set out for that abode; and by the guidance of the sparrow betook themselves to the vicinity of the hawk's nest. Now the hawk, with his children, thoughtless of such a calamity, had eaten plentifully, and were gone to sleep. The salamanders, having scattered all the naphtha and brimstone which they had with them, over their nest, turned back: and the wind of divine justice having blown, the flame of wrath fell upon the nest of that oppressor. They rose up from the sleep of negligence, at a time when the hand of remedy was unequal to the extinction of that flame; and the whole of them, at once, with home and nest, became ashes. *Couplet.*—

"A tyrant, by violence, kindled a fire once; when it threw up a blaze, it first burnt even him."

Now I have told this story, that thou mayest know that every person who labours in the repulse of an enemy, although he be small and weak, and the enemy great and powerful, there is hope of aid and victory.

Kalīlah said. Now that the lion has given him distinction from among the rest, and has exalted the banner of his fortune, to pluck out attachment to him, from the heart of the lion, and to change the disposition of the lion towards him, seems extremely difficult: for kings, when they cherish any one, do not disgrace him without some thorough reason; and whomsoever they raise up, they do not cast down from their regard, unless some great affair should occur. *Couplet.*—"The water will not carry down the wood; what is the reason? it would be ashamed to bear down that which is nourished by itself." Damanah said. What cause can be more complete than this, that the king has shewn an excess in cherishing him, and indulged contempt for his other counsellors, till, of course they have become disgusted with his service; and the benefits of their duty, and the advantages of their advice, have been cut off from him: and from this state of things great calamities are to be anticipated. For philosophers have said, that danger to a king and misfortune to a country may be by one of six things. First,—Alienation: that is to say, making well-wishers disappointed with himself, and abandoning people of judgment and experience in disgrace. Second,—Strife: which is such, that wars without object, and inconsiderate undertakings take place, and the swords of opponents are drawn from the scabbard. Third,—Pleasure: and that is the being attached to women; having a fondness for hunting; being engaged in wine; and having an inclination for play and amusement. Fourth,—The enmity of fortune: and that is some event, which occurs in time; as pestilence, famine, earthquakes, burnings, inundations, and the like. Fifth,—Violence of temper; which is excess in exercising anger: and to go to an extreme in punishment and chastisement. Sixth,—Ignorance: which is such, that in a fit time for peace he is disposed to war; and in a fit occasion for war he shews an inclination for peace; and in the time for gentleness he chooses contention; and when he ought to close up the rampart of anger, he sets open the gate of kindness. *Couplet.*—"War and peace, out of season, do not come to any use: in the place for flowers, be flowers; and in the place for thorns, thorns."

Kalīlah said. I have perceived that thou hast bound up the loins for revenge; and art seated in ambush for Shanzabah; and thou desirest that by thy intervention some evil may happen to him. But I know that to inflict injury has no good consequence; and that, in the way of retribution, the mischief of every man turns back upon him. *Couplet.*—"Whoever did evil, saw nothing but evil; the mischief of it soon came upon him." For whoever will open the eyes of experience, and will observe the retribution of evil and good, there is doubt but he will hold to the side of goodness and gentleness; and will preserve his hand and tongue from vexation and injury: as the king, the dispenser of justice, remarked.

Kalīlah said. I have heard that in former times there was a king who had spread out the hand of violence and aggression, and had put forth the foot of perverseness from the path of justice and liberality. *Couplet.*—"World-burner; merciless; displaying pride; by his bitterness the face of a world sour." The people night and day, had lifted up their hands in prayer against his injustice; and had loosened the tongue of hatred. One day, this king went to the chase, and when he came back, he ordered a proclamation, thus—O men! the eye of my heart has been veiled till this day, from the sight of the face of rectitude; and the hand of my sin hath drawn the sword of cruelty in the face of the disappointed, suffering violence, and of the oppressed, come to trouble. Now, I am become sincere in the post of protecting the people, and stedfast in the office of extending justice. There is a hope of this, that after this day, the hand of any tyrant shall not strike the ring of vexation on the door of the house of any peasant; and that the foot of any dealer in violence shall not reach the court of the dwelling of any poor man. *Couplet.*—" Do not expect ease in that border and land; where thou seest the people heart-light with the king." A new life burst forth to the people at this news; and at these tidings, the flower of desire blossomed to the poor in the garden of hope. *Couplet.*—"At these blessed tidings which came suddenly, a glad message came to the heart and a joyful sound to the soul."

To the Story. The happy influence of his justice came to such a point that the lamb would drink milk from the dugs of the fierce lion; and the pheasant was a play-fellow with the hawk, on common ground; and on this account they gave him the title, *The king, doing justice.* *Couplet.* —" He made the foundations of equity so firm, that fire became a watchman to sulphur."

One of the familiar confidential men of the government, in a moment of opportunity, put a question about the particulars of the case, and sought an explanation of the change of the bitterness of force and cruelty for the gentleness of favour and duty. The king replied thus: The day that I went a hunting, I was galloping on every side: on a sudden I saw that a dog ran in pursuit of a fox, and with his teeth bit through the bone of his leg; the helpless fox, with his lame leg fled away into a hole; and the dog turned back: at that moment a footman flung a stone and broke the leg of that dog; as yet, he had not gone many steps, when a horse kicked the footman, and his leg was broken; and the horse, too, not having cleared a bit of the way, his foot went down into a hole and broke.

I came to myself, and said, hast thou seen what they did and what they suffered? whoever does what he ought not, feels what he would not. *Verses.*—"Find out good; do not evil; beware: for thou shalt again meet with evil and good; if in all places thou art disposed to goodness, thou shalt find thyself exalted; but, if thou go in the path of evil, thou shalt behold thyself trampled under the foot of want."

Now I have hit off this fable, that thou shouldest reflect upon retribution; and depart from the ground of malevolence: may it not be, that the ignominy of it should reach to thee, and that the meaning of this, "whoever dug a well for his brother, why truly he fell into it," should display brightness. And an eminent man hath said, do not evil, lest thou fall into evil; dig not a well, lest thou fall in thyself.

Damanah replied, I, in this occurrence, am the oppressed, not the tyrant; I bear the violence, and am not the doer of violence; and if the injured man be in the design of revenge against the oppressor, what retribution will there be for that; and if any hurt should come from him to his tormenter, what harm will be consequent upon that.

Kalīlah said, I have allowed that in this proceeding, no mischief may find a way into thy affairs; but yet, in what manner canst thou labour for the destruction of the ox; whilst he has strength superior to thy strength; and his friends and allies are more than thy friends and adherents.

Damanah said, One should not lay the foundations of affairs upon great strength, and countless assistants; but should prefer skill and contrivance before them; for whatever men do by skill and stratagem, the probability is that it would not succeed by force and strength: and has it never reached thee, how a raven destroyed a snake by stratagem?

Kalīlah said, how was that?

STORY.

He replied, They have related that a raven had fixed her abode in the middle of a mountain, and had made her nest in the cleft of a rock; and in the vicinity of it was the hole of a snake, the water of whose mouth might be destructive and deadly poison, and the saliva of the roots of his teeth would be destructive of the constitution of perpetuity and life. Whenever the raven deposited her young, the snake would eat them; and used to burn the liver of the raven with the brand of the loss of her offspring. When the cruelty of the snake was gone beyond limit, the worn-out raven communicated the complaint of that condition to a jackal, who was her friend, and said, I am thinking how I shall extricate myself from the calamity of the snake, and from the evil of this life-hunting tyrant. The jackal asked, In what way wilt thou advance in this emergency? and by what art wilt thou avert his mischief? The raven replied, I mean, that when the snake is gone to sleep, I will dig out his world-seeing eyes, with my blood-drinking beak; that he may not again be able to make an attack upon my joy of the eye; and that my children, which are the light of my eye, may be left safe from the wickedness of that malicious look.

The jackal said, This scheme is wide of the track of right conduct: for it behoves prudent men to make an attack upon an enemy by some method, in which there may be no danger of life. Beware: depart from this thought, that thou mayest not ruin thyself, like the heron, who exerted himself to destroy the crab, and gave his own dear life to the winds.

The raven said, how happened that?

STORY.

The jackal said. There was a heron, dwelling upon the bank of a certain piece of water; and of all objects the purport of his heart was turned to fishing; and he used to catch fish, to the extent of his wants, and pass his life in comfort: when the weakness of old age made way upon him, and his bodily faculties were inclined to give way, being unequal to the pursuit of fish, and being caught in the snare of grief, he said to himself, *Couplet.*—"Alas! the caravan of life! for it is gone so far, that their dust has not reached the air of our country." Alas! for I have flung precious life to the winds, in trifling sports: I have not laid up in store any thing which in the season of old age may afford any traces of manhood, or give me any support: and at this day there is not any strength left, and there is no amends for strength: that will be best, that I build my conduct upon stratagem, and spread out the net of device and deceit; it may be that, by this subterfuge, life may go on. So he sat down upon the brink of the water, like those who weep and sigh, and make lamentation. A certain crab espied him afar off; she came forward, and having thrown out the first forms of familiar talk, said. My dear sir, I find thee melancholy; what is the reason of it? He replied. How shall I not be sorrowful? And thou dost not know that the source of my maintenance, and the stock of my living was this; that every day I used to catch a fish or two, and hence there would result to me a check to the last gasp, food to stop death: there was no great loss to the fish from this; and my days were decked in the ornament of contentment and gladness. To-day, two sportsmen were passing along here and saying, that there were a great many fish in this lake, and that some contrivance must be made for them. One of them said. In such and such a lake the fish are more numerous than this; let us first settle their business, and then turn our views upon these. Now if the matter is to be in this fashion, I must tear up my heart from sweet life, and fix it upon the bitterness of death. The crab, when she heard this news, instantly returned, and went up to the fishes, and related the alarming intelligence, just as she had heard it. Agitation and clamour broke out amongst them; and in union with the crab they set their faces to the heron, and said. Such a piece of news has reached us from thee, and borne away the reins of contrivance from our hands. *Couplet.*—" The more we look upon the emergency, from head to foot, the more, like the compasses, are we giddy." Now we consult with thee. He who is consulted is trustworthy. A wise man, although it were an enemy, when they consult with him, it behoves him that he should not lay aside the conditions of advice; and especially in an affair where the advantage may revert to him. Now thou dost thyself acknowledge that the continuance of thy being is wrapped up in us: and that thy life is dependent upon our existence: so what dost thou think right in our concerns?

The heron answered thus. I heard these words myself from the tongue of the fishermen; and resistance against them cannot take any shape: nor does any device but this occur to my mind. I know a lake, close by, whose water breathes equality in clearness with the pure dawn; and in reflecting forms takes precedence of the mirror, displaying the world: one can count the grains of sand at the bottom of it, and see the eggs of the fish in its basin: and yet withal neither can the diver of comprehension reach to its depth; nor the traveller of the fancy perceive its shore; the eye of the snare of any sportsman hath not fallen on that lake; and the fish of that pool have not known any imprisonment but a chain of water. *Couplet.*—" It is a lake in the likeness of an ocean; but it is an ocean without end or bottom." If ye could remove to that place, ye might be in safety and repose, in enjoyment and tranquility, for the remainder of life. They said, It is a good notion; but our removal is not possible without thy help and aid. The heron replied, I should not begrudge you whatever I may have of strength and power; but the time is short; the fisherman may come from hour to hour, and the opportunity be lost. The fish supplicated; and as a great favour, the determination settled upon this; that every day having taken up several fish, he should carry them to that lake. So every morning the heron used to take away several fish, and eat them on the top of the hillock that was in the neighbourhood. And when he used to come back, the others would make haste for the removal and change; and seek for advance and precedence over one another. Wisdom looked upon their folly and negligence with the eye of example; and time, with a thousand eyes, wept over their lamentable condition. And doubtless, every one who is beguiled by the flattery of an enemy, and holds as proper reliance upon a base person, mean in race, his deserts are this.

When many days had passed, a fancy for that lake having got into the head of a crab also, he wanted to remove; and gave the heron knowledge of the idea. The heron reflected thus: There is not a more thorough enemy to me than he; the best thing is this, that I convey him away also to his friends. So he advanced, and having taken the crab upon his neck, he set off for the bed-chamber of the fish. The crab, who saw the bones of the fish from afar, understood how the matter was, and considered with himself thus: a sensible man, when he sees that an enemy has a design upon his life, if he neglects exertion will have toiled in his own blood; and when he shall strive, his condition will not go beyond two things; if he becomes victorious, he leaves a reputation for courage upon the page of time; or if the business should not prosper, at least he is not reproached for want of spirit and self-defence. *Fragment.*—"When an enemy has attacked thee, in order to repel the injury, strive with zeal and energy, if thou art distinguished by reason; for if thy desire comes to hand, thou reachest thy wish; and if it does not come about, thou art then excused." Then the crab cast himself about the neck of the heron, and began to squeeze his throat tight. The heron was old and feeble, and becoming senseless with the least pressure on his throat, he fell down from the air, and became even with the dust. The crab having alighted from his neck, took his own fancy; and having set his foot on the way, came to the rest of the fish, and mingling condolence for departed friends with congratulations on the life of those present, gave them information of the state of the case. The whole being delighted, reckoned on the death of the heron as a new existence, and a life without measure. *Verses.*—"One moment of life, after the death of such an enemy, I have a notion it is better than a century of existence: we do not exult over the death of our enemy; but then one moment of separation from an enemy is better than thou canst name."

And I have struck off this copy, that thou mayest understand that many a man goes to ruin by his own deceit and cunning; and that the mischief of his treachery, according to this text, "base fraud does not take effect, except upon its author," turns round upon himself. But I will show thee a method, which if you act upon it, may be the cause of thy security, and the ruin of thine enemy. The raven said. It is not possible to depart from the directions of friends, nor to oppose the judgment of the wise. *Couplet.*—"Thou guidest me, cup-bearer, to the wine-house: opposition to thy will is not the path of affection." The jackal said. The best thing is this; that thou take flight to the top of the air, and cast thy sight upon the terraces of the houses and the plains; and wherever thou seest any jewellery, the seizure of which may be practicable, having come down, thou shalt take it up, and fly into the open space of the air, in such a way that thou be not lost from the sight of the people; for there is no doubt but some men will come upon the track, in pursuit of the ornament; and when thou shalt come near the snake drop it down upon him, that to those people the sight may fall upon him: certainly, having first let him loose from the bondage of life, they will take up the jewels; and thy heart shall find rest, without thyself having made any exertion to get rid of him. The raven, at the suggestion of the jackal, set off for inhabited places; she saw a woman, who having laid her ornaments in a corner of the terrace, was herself occupied in her ablutions; these the raven carried off, and just in the manner that the jackal had said, threw them on the snake. The men who had come on the track of the raven, instantly beat his head to pieces: and the raven escaped free. *Hemistich.*—"The enemy went from the midst, and the tears also from the bosom."

Damanah said. I have told this tale, that thou mayest know that what it is possible to do by cunning, may not be possible by strength. Kalīlah said. To the ox strength and fierceness, reason and management, all abound; and by stratagem, it is not possible to get the better of such a person; for on every side, where thou by stratagem shall effect an opening, he by thought will close it up; and it is likely that before thou shalt make a supper upon him, he will make a breakfast off thee. Perhaps the story of that hare has never come to thy ears, who formed the purpose of entrapping the fox, and got caught herself.

Damanah said, how was that?

STORY.

Kalīlah said. I have heard that a hungry wolf was running along a plain, on the scent of a meal; he saw a hare, asleep, in the shade of a bush; and the sleep of negligence had seized upon all parts of her. The wolf reckoned her an immense booty, and began to advance slowly towards her. The hare, being warned by the alarm of his breath, and the dread of his step, jumped up, and wanted to run away. The wolf, having got possession of the road, said. *Couplet.*—"Come on, come on; for I have no power to bear distance: go not, go not; for I am in despair by absence." The hare stood still on the spot, with awe of him; and having begun to supplicate, rubbed the face of entreaty on the earth, and said, I know that the fire of the hunger of the prince of beasts is in a blaze; and that the faculty of nutrition, by reason of the search of food, is in agitation: yet I, with this feeble frame and weak body, am no more than one mouthful for the prince: what is the good of me; by eating me up, what can be made secure, or what set free? There is in this neighbourhood a fox, who from excess of fatness cannot travel; and from abundance of flesh is not able to move. Somehow, I think that his flesh, in juice and freshness, is like the water of life; and his blood, in sweetness and delicacy, like sherbet of sugar-candy. If the prince would give his feet the trouble, I would, by any stratagem that I can, bring him into captivity, and the prince may just break his fast upon him: if any pleasure should arise, why there it is; and if not, I am still your prisoner and captive. Get others into the noose; for we ourselves are captive. The wolf being deluded by his false and juggling words, followed the path to the dwelling of the fox. Now there was in that neighbourhood a fox, who in deceitfulness might have read a lecture to Satan; and who, in forming devices and playing tricks, might have given a lesson to fancy and imagination. *Verses.*—" He was a little fox, alert and hypocritical; or if not, he was the lord of that wilderness: he was a sprite, the conjuror of the plains and the village; and in his subtlety had carried off the victory from all the beasts: both the beasts of the plains were lamenting about him; and the dogs of the village were howling against him: at the moment of leaping, he became lost from view, having swept the court of the sky with the broom of his tail."

The hare had an old quarrel with him: upon this occasion, having found an opportunity, he formed the design of revenge: so having left the wolf at the entrance of the hole, he entered the abode of the fox, and fulfilled the customs of salutation and good wishes. The fox, too, with great deference, returned an answer to the salutation, and said. *Couplet.*—" Thou art welcome; whence comest thou? come in; sit down: come in; for I will give thee a place upon my face and my eyes; sit down. The hare said. For a long time since I am always in anxiety for the honour of an interview; and am disappointed of that happiness by the impediments of treacherous fortune, and the accidents of a faithless and inconstant age; but lately a holy man, who in the Egypt of divine favour is exalted to sovereignty, and in the regions of spiritual power is a sage indulgent to disciples, has done us the honour to come to this country from the sacred shrine: and having heard the fame of the monastic seclusion and retirement of your lordship, has made your humble slave a means of introduction, that he may enlighten the eye of his heart with that world-adorning beauty, and perfume the palate of his soul with the odours of your musk-like thoughts: if there be permission for a meeting, then good; but if the time does not allow it, some other chance may occur. *Couplet.*—" Either let him go back from this gate, like unforeseen calamities: or let him alight upon this place, like the prayer that is accepted."

The fox read off, from the page of this discourse, a picture of stratagem; and contemplated in the mirror of these words the image of a deceitful scheme. He said to himself. The wisest thing is this; that I should proceed with them, just in their own fashion; and just pour down their throats some of their own draughts. A stone is the recompence of him who flings stones. So the fox, too, set a great deal of flattery to work; and said. We have girded up the loins in the service of travellers for this purpose; and have opened the door of the cell in the face of holy men—for the sake of this—that we may derive a benefit from the sublimity of their state of extacy, and from their excellent thoughts; especially such a holy man as thou dost represent: and to this kind of eminent person, whom thou dost describe, what deficiency can I show in hospitality, or what minute point can I neglect in humble duty? For "the guest when he alights, alights to his own appointed food;" and our ancestors have said. *Fragment.*—"Whomsoever thou mayest see in the world is eating his own daily bread; whether his bread be from thy board, or from his own board: therefore it behoves thee to receive a favour from a guest, because he eats, at the board of thy abundance, his own bread." But I entertain a hope that thou wilt make some delay, that I may draw a broom over this corner of a nest; and that, for the sake of this guest of holy steps, I may spread a carpet which may be worthy of the occasion. The hare imagined that his invention having taken with the fox, he would instantly have the honour of waiting upon the wolf. He replied. The guest is a man without ceremony, and simple in character; and has an indifference to finery of lodging and clothing: but since your transcendent mind desires to observe some ceremony, there is no harm neither in that; go to the business. He said this, and came out and communicated the whole occurrence to the wolf; and gave him glad tidings of the fox having been deluded: and then in repetition, for in every novelty there is a pleasure, he began to praise the flesh, and the fat, the juiciness and freshness of the fox. While the wolf, having sharpened the teeth of appetite, was sweetening his mouth with the relish of the flesh of the fox; and the hare, because of this good service, was forming with himself a notion of freedom. But the fox, from views of caution and foresight, prior to this by a long time, had dug a deep pit in his dwelling, and gradually carried out all the earth of it; and had covered the top of it with a little rubbish and bushes; and he had also a secret way, by which, in time of necessity, he could get out from there. When he had dispatched the hare he came to the edge of the pit, and arranged the rubbish and bushes of it in such a manner, that it would sink on a slight movement. Then coming to the mouth of the secret path, he called out thus. O venerable guests, give your feet the trouble. And in the moment of their entrance, he departed by that opening. The hare, with prodigious alacrity, and the wolf, with thorough greediness, walked into that dark cell. To step upon the edge of the rubbish, and to tumble to the bottom of the pit, was the same thing. The wolf fancied that this trick, too, was one of the hare's doings; he instantly tore her in pieces, and relieved the world from the disgrace of her existence.

And I have produced this instance, that thou shouldest understand that stratagem will not advance with clever men; and that a person who has any share of caution and forethought, does not grow conceited by the delusions of any one.

Damanah replied. It is as thou sayest: but the ox is conceited of himself, and is inattentive to my animosity; and I can overthrow him by his negligence: for the treacherous arrow, which they let fly from the ambush of friendship, is the more penetrating. Perhaps thou hast not heard in what way the treachery of the hare became effectual upon the lion; and that since he was inattentive to the fraud, notwithstanding his sagacity and penetration, he fell into the labyrinth of ruin.

Kalīlah said, how was that?

STORY.

Damanah said. They have related that in the vicinity of Bagdad there was a meadow, whose breezes might perfume the odour of paradise; and the lustre of whose sweet herbs might enlighten the eye of the sky: from each branch of its flowery banks a thousand stars were shining; and in the beauty of every one of those stars nine spheres revolving. *Verses.*—" Flowing streams, through herbage fed on moisture; like quicksilver, through a statue of lapis lazuli: sweet herbs sprouted up on the banks of the stream; the gales shedding amber; the air smelling of musk."

Now in that meadow there were many harmless animals; and by means of the goodness of the climate, the delightfulness of the position, the plenty of water, and the vastness of the abundance, they used to pass the time in pleasure and comfort. But in the neighbourhood was a fierce-tempered mischief-seeking lion; who used every day to exhibit to those helpless creatures an unpropitious meeting; and made enjoyment and existence disagreeable to them. One day, having come to the agreement, they went to the lion; and having set forth their allegiance and obedience, they said, O king! we are thy subjects and attendants; and thou, every day, after vast pains and boundless trouble, art able to hunt down one of us, or not: while we are constantly, from dread of thee, under a struggle of misfortune; and thou also, in the pursuit of us, art in a chase after sorrow. We have just now made a scheme, which may be a means of tranquility to thee, and a cause of security and rest to us. If, as heretofore, thou wilt not be vexatious to us, and wilt not daily make our time miserable, we will send a head of game, at breakfast time, as a daily provision for the kitchen of the king; nor will we allow any deficiency in the delivery of it. The lion gave his consent to it. And they, every day, used to cast lots; and in the name of whomsoever of the animals it came up, they would send him to the lion for the purpose of the daily supply; till in this manner some time had elapsed. One day the lot came forth in the name of the hare; and the times made her the target of the arrow of evil. She said to her friends. If you will show a little forbearance towards me, in sending me, I will extricate you from the oppression of this tyrant. They replied. On this point there is no harm. The hare for an hour made delay, till the time of breakfast was gone by; and the ferocious nature of the lion having come into action, he was grinding his teeth together, in a rage with the animals. The hare went very softly towards him, and found him exceedingly vexed; the fire of hunger having seated him upon the wind, and the glare of anger being manifest in each movement and attitude. *Couplet.*—"The oven of the stomach, every moment heating; would be a calamity on the day of not finding." The hare found the lion, from excess of rage, beating his tail, in vengeance, on the ground; and seeking, with anxiety of mind, an infringement of the treaty. He advanced slowly, and made a salutation. The lion enquired, whence comest thou? and what is the matter with the beasts? She said. According to established custom, they had sent a hare in company with me; and by mutual consent, we had the design of attendance: a lion came up with us on the way, and snatched her up; and though we used vehemence, saying it was the food of the king of the harmless animals, and the daily supply of their monarch, he paid no attention to my words, but said, this is my hunting ground; and the game of it belongs to me: thou hast not heard, perhaps, "every lion and his own woods." O king, having set forth pride and boasting, he so explained the power of his might, that I became at a loss, and have fled from before him, that I might lay the state of the case open to your enlightened mind. The haughtiness of ignorance being excited in the lion, he said. *Verses.*—"I am one who, in the art of taunts and blows, will teach among lions the rules of war: what lion shall show this daring, that he casts his paw upon my prey?" Then he said. O hare! canst thou show him to me, that I might do justice to thy heart against him, and also reap my own revenge? The hare said. Why should not I be able, when he has uttered all sorts of disrespectful expressions with respect to the king: and if I had been able, I would have made the cup of his head a water trough for the beasts of the field.

Couplet.—" But I trust in God, that I shall see him in thy clutches; to my heart's desire." She said this, and put herself in advance; and the simple-hearted lion, beguiled by her fraud, began to move on behind her.

The hare led the lion to the brink of a large well, whose water, by its clearness, like a mirror of China, would represent all forms correctly; and would, without mistake, tell the character of the dress, and the countenance of each of the beholders. *Couplet.*—" No one ever looked into it; but he perused his own image from the page of its brilliant mind." She said. O king! thy worthless enemy is in this well; and I am frightened at his awfulness: if your majesty would take me into his bosom, I could show the enemy to him. The lion having taken her into his bosom, looked down into the well, and saw the image of himself and the hare in the water. He thought it was that lion, and that he had dragged to his breast the hare which had been his daily supply. He dropped her, and threw himself into the well; and after two or three plunges gave up his blood-thirsty soul to the flames of hell. And the hare, returning in safety, gave the animals intelligence of the particulars of the event: and they shewing constancy in the daily duty of thankfulness to God, went on grazing at ease in gardens of security and peace; and used to repeat this *Couplet.*—" A single draught of water, after sad thoughts, is pleasanter than a life of seventy years."

In producing this example, it is understood, that an enemy, however powerful he may be, in a state of carelessness, it is possible to get the advantage over him. Kalīlah said. If thou shouldst be able to ruin the ox, so that any vexation may not reach the lion, it might have some shew, and one might, in some sort excuse it; but if his destruction should not succeed without injury to the lion, take care that thou set not about the business: for a sensible person will not choose inconvenience to one whom he serves, for the sake of his own comfort. The conversation, at these words, came to an end: and Damanah, having abstained from attendance, went into the corner of seclusion; till one day, having found an opportunity, he thrust himself in private upon the lion, and stood, like one that is sorrowful and grieved, with a sore mind, and his head down. The lion said. It is many days that I have not seen thee: is it well? He replied. Please God, in future, it may be well. The lion was startled, and said Has anything happened? He said yes. He said. Relate it. Damanah answered. There must be a private place, and a leisure time for that. The lion replied. This moment is the time; explain it quickly, for important affairs do not endure delay: and if the business of to-day falls upon to-morrow, a thousand evils may appear *Couplet.*—"Make no delay; but bring forward the chief point of the business: for in delay there are many evils." Damanah said. Every word, on hearing which, aversion may happen to the hearer; in relating those things, one should shew boldness; and it is not fit to repeat them, except upon much thought and great consideration; unless there be perfect confidence in the reason and discrimination of the hearer; and he who hears them also should consider the circumstances of the speaker; whether he is in a position for advice and well-wishing, or not; and when he knows that the speaker can have no object but the discharge of the claims of patronage, he ought to shew attention to his words, with the ear of consent; especially when the benefits and advantages of them revert back to him. The lion said. Thou dost know that I am become an exception from kings, by the superiority of my judgment, and the excellency of my prudence; and that in listening to the language of every person, I make royal discrimination the model of my mind: do thou say whatever thou wilt, without ceremony; and without hesitation do not keep secret whatever may have come to thy mind. Damanah said. I also have obtained permission for this boldness, on this account, that my confidence is to the utmost settled upon the wisdom and knowledge of your majesty; and besides it is not concealed, that I utter my words out of pure affection, and the essence of honesty; and do not pollute them with mistrust and doubt, or with design and motives: and nothing but the touchstone of the imperial nature ascertains the standard of the coin of words. *Couplet.*—" Praise to God! that the understanding of the king is a touchstone; which can ascertain our alloy and our pureness." The lion replied. The fulness of thy honesty is manifest; and the remarks of it are clear on the forehead of thy habits; and without reserve, thy words become imputed to affection and advice; while suspicion and doubt find no place of entrance about them. Damanah said. The preservation of the whole mass of animals is bound up with the life of your majesty; it therefore behoves every one of the subjects who is endued and distinguished by the marks of pure disposition, and genuine descent, that he withhold nothing from the king, in the discharge of duty, and declaration of the sincerity of advice: for philosophers have said, that whoever conceals any right from the king, or any infirmity from the physician, or who does not see fit to expose his poverty and want to his friends, will have committed treachery to himself. The lion said. Thy attachment and singleness of mind have been long ago apparent to me; and I have known thy honesty and integrity: now tell me what has happened, that after a knowledge of the particulars of the case, occupation may proceed with the management of it. Damanah, when he had deluded and deceived the lion with his canting and cheating, let loose his tongue, and said. *Couplet.*—" O king! may discretion be thy guide; victory thy friend; and enemies thy contempt." Shanzabah has had many private interviews with the generals of the army; and has introduced conversations with the pillars of the state; and has said thus. I have tried the lion; and have learnt the measure of his strength and power, and judgment and sagacity; and in each have observed many defects, and innumerable weakness. *Couplet.*—"He was not such, as he was to us in idea; we had a great notion of him, but he was no such thing." And I am in amazement, that your majesty, in honouring this treacherous denier of munificence, shewed all that excess; and made him the second of two, in power and authority; in return for all that favour, this idea has come into being from him; and in opposition to so much kindness, this design has thrust out its head from his character. But to a certainty, in conformity with—verily man is rebellious, if his will be independent—the person who sees his hands unshackled in commanding and forbidding, and finds the reins of loosening and binding general affairs in the grasp of his own authority—the demon of strife will lay eggs in the nest of his brain; and the lust of wickedness will burst forth from the blackness of his heart. *Verses.*—"The man whom the world shall raise up from the well of contempt, and carry to the summit of admiration; it were a wonder, if he should not make a claim to sovereignty; or throw the heads of the rebellious into the noose." The lion said, O Damanah! consider well what words these are which thou speakest, and whence thou hast learnt the particulars of this circumstance: and if it be, as is understood from thy declaration, of what sort the management of it should be. Damanah said, The exaltation of his rank, and the elevation of his station, are clear to your majesty. And when a king sees any one of his servants in competition with himself in degree of honour, wealth, and pomp, he should the more quickly remove him from his presence, or else the business will get out of his hands; and the king will fall from his position. And the remedy for this matter, in such wise as the enlightened mind, the shelter of government may dictate—where can our languid thoughts, and deficient talents reach to it. I am sure, however, that arrangements in this affair ought to be made with promptitude; and that if you deliberate, it is possible the matter may come to that point, that the fool of management will be unequal to the extent of its management. *Fragment.*—"Thy enemy was only an ant; it became a snake: pick out the brains from this ant, grown to a snake: give him not time, any longer; do not carry on life: for he becomes a dragon, if a snake finds time." And they have said that men are of two classes: the man of caution, and the inefficient man: the inefficient is one who, at the time of the occurrence of an event, or the falling out of any accident, is confused in head, distracted, agitated in manner, and wandering; while the man of caution is one who, having followed forethought, is always considering the consequences of affairs. Men of caution, also, are of two kinds. First, he who, before the appearance of the danger, shall have recognized the quality of it; and that which others learn in the termination of affairs, he, in the commencement of them, shall have seen with the eye of reason; and who shall have provided for the conclusions of matters, in the beginnings. *Verses.*—"First thought; last action." And such a person, before he shall fall into the whirlpool of calamity, is able to convey himself to the shore of freedom: and him they call most cautious. And the second is one who, when misfortune comes, keeping his courage steady, does not give way to consternation and alarm: and, doubtless, to such a person the path of right conduct, and the means of management, will not be concealed: and this man they call cautious. And applicable to the condition of these three persons (of whom one is perfectly wise, and another half wise, and the third a negligent fool,) is the story of those three fish who had fallen together in a pond. The lion asked in what way was that?

STORY.

Damanah said, They have related that there was a lake

far from the high road, hidden, and concealed from the passage of travellers: its water pure, like the faith of the spiritual; its appearance, gratifying to those who were looking for the fountain of immortality; and the lake communicated with the running stream. And three huge fishes there reposed: Pisces, in jealousy of them, would burn upon the pan of envy, like Aries under the heat of the sun: one of them was *most cautious;* another, *cautious;* and the other, *helpless.* Suddenly, in the season of spring, when the world, from the splendour of the garden, had become a pattern of Paradise, and where all parts of the expanse of the earth, with its sparkling herbs, were like the azure vault, full of stars; when the chamberlain, the morning breeze, had adorned the floor of the earth with variegated couplets; and the matchless gardener of creation had ornamented the garden of the world with flowers of various hues. *Verses.*—"The garden was loaded with musk by the breeze of the moon; the jessamine, in its delicacy, like the cheek of our beloved; at the breath of the dawn, the rose opened her lips, like a smiling beauty encouraging her lover."

Suddenly, the way of two or three fishermen chanced to be by that lake. Providentially, they fully discovered the circumstance of the abode of the three fish in the lake; so they made an appointment together, and ran to fetch a net. The fishes, being aware of the occurrence, fell into company with the fire of anguish, in the very heart of the water. When night came on, that fish which was perfectly wise, and professed the most caution, because he had many times seen the assault of the treacherous times, and the insolent looks of the indiscriminate sky, and had always stood firm on the floor of experience, began to turn in his mind the thought of escape from the net of the fishermen, and the idea of liberation from their capture. *Verses.*—"Recognise that man as prudent and wise, who lays a solid foundation for all his proceedings; the man whose caution is not firm, the foundation of all his designs will be very weak." So he set his face briskly to the work, and, or ever he made any consultation with his friends, got out on that side where it was connected with the river. At dawn, the fishermen, making their appearance, firmly secured the two ends of the lake; and the half-clever fish, who was distinguished by the ornament of prudence, but had no share of the stores of prudence, when he observed the circumstance, felt great shame, and said, I have given way to supineness, and such is the conclusion of the affairs of the negligent; it would have been right that I, like that fish, should have tasted my trouble, before the arrival of the misfortune; and should have thought of escape, before the attack of calamity. *Couplet.*—" The remedy for an occurrence should be made before the event; neglect does no good when the affair has got beyond our reach."

Now that the opportunity of flight has been lost, is the season for deceit and stratagem. Though they have said, that arrangements in a time of distress, do not yield much advantage; and that much enjoyment does not arise from the fruit of skill in the season of calamity; yet, with all this, it behoves a wise man that he should, on no account, despair of the benefits of wisdom; and should never admit of delay or tardiness in repelling the devices of an enemy. So he feigned himself dead, and went floating on the surface of the water. One of the fishermen picked him up; and, under the notion of his being dead, flung him on the bare ground; and he, by a trick, threw himself into the river, and saved his life. *Couplet.*—" Die, my friend, if thou desirest freedom; for without dying, thou canst not find thy friend."

But the other fish, in whose habits supineness was predominant, and weakness manifest in all his actions, went about, right and left, astounded, confused, delirious, and unsteady; and kept looking to the surface, and to the bottom, until at last he was caught.

And from the relation of this fable, it will appear certain to the king, that speed must be used in the matter of Shanzabah; and that, before the loss of opportunity and power, he should, with a sword of high temper, strike the fire of remorse into the soul of that vile dust,—give the granary of his life to the wind of destruction,—and send up the smoke of his lineage to the sky. *Couplet.*—"Whilst power still remains over the treacherous foe, dash out his brains with the stone of desolation."

The lion replied, What thou hast said, has been understood; but I have no suspicion that Shanzabah meditates any dishonesty, or that he will allow the sure results of ingratitude to stand in opposition to my past acts of bounty; for, in all this time, I have never held any thing to be right towards him, but goodness and kindness.

Damanah said, It is even so; but it is these favours of the king, which has raised him to this elevation. *Couplet.*—"It is for thee to say, where the scar shall be; and since thou layest on the ointment, what does it signify?"

An abject fellow, of a base spirit, will be of one mind and give good advice, all the time that he has not reached the station of which he is in hopes; but when his object is attained, a desire for other degrees of elevation, for which he has no fitness, will burst forth from the treasury of his fancy. And the ancients have said, that the duty of a base and low-born man depends upon the rule of fear and hope: where he is secure against the effects of fear, he darkens the fountain head of loyalty; and where, by the attainment of all his hopes, he feels self-sufficient, he kindles the fire of ingratitude and disturbance. The lion said, Then, in what way can one proceed with servants of a base disposition, and of low sentiments; so that vestiges of ingratitude may not become manifest? Damanah answered, One should not so far deprive them of one's favours, that becoming all at once hopeless, and quitting our service, they shall incline to our enemies; nor yet should we bestow such bounty and wealth upon them, that having attained to the limits of prosperity, extravagant fancies may burst out in them: but they should rather always live between fear and hope; and all their undertakings should turn upon the promises and threats of fear and hope. For power and security will render them self-sufficient; and that may be a means of rebellion and offence: despair and misery will make servants audacious; and that becomes a cause of injury to the dignity of kings. *Couplet.*—" The hopeless man becomes daring and insolent of speech; Oh! my friend, do not act so that I shall become hopeless."

The lion replied, To my mind it seems, that the mirror of Shanzabah's character is quite clear of the rust of this deceit; and that the page of his heart is pure and free from the writing of such a fancy; for I have always been upon a footing of indulgence to him; I have even made my favours to mingle with his fortune: and after kindness and benefits have constantly overtaken him from me, how can he meditate harm and injury in return for this? *Couplet.*—" Since my heart makes itself conspicuous by love for him, why should he raise the standard in enmity to me?"

Damanah said, The king ought to know that truth can never proceed from those who are crooked in temper; and that one of an evil disposition, and of a corrupt stock, will never, nor by the exertions of others, nor by his own efforts, become amiable in temper, or virtuous in character. " Every pot leaks with what is in it." *Verse.*—" The same thing trickles out from the pitcher that is within." Perhaps the story of the scorpion and the tortoise may not have reached the august hearing of your majesty.

The lion enquired what it was; and Damanah said,

Story.

A tortoise had an attachment to a scorpion; they were ever breathing the air of unanimity, and forming plans of concord. *Couplet.*—"From morn to night, united and intimate; from eve till dawn, associates and confidential." It happened on a time, that by reason of some necessity, it would be necessary to abandon their native spot; and so the two set off, in company with each other, for another habitation. By chance their way lay across a vast river, and a great stream of water appeared across their path; and since the passage of the scorpion across the water was out of the question, he fell back in amaze. The tortoise said, My dear friend, what has come to you, that you have given the collar of the garment of life into the hand of melancholy, and have gathered up the skirt of your heart from joy and gladness? The scorpion said, My brother! the thought about getting over this water has thrown me into a whirlpool of consternation; neither the passage over the river is to be accomplished; nor to sustain separation from my friends possible. *Couplet.*—"Thou goest on, whilst I, desolate, remain behind; how that I should endure without thee; a wonder that I should remain at all." The tortoise said, Don't suffer any pain; for I, carrying you without the least trouble over the water, will land you on the bank; and turning my back into a boat, I will make a breast thy buckler against calamity; it would be a pity, with difficulty to gain a friend, and with coolness give him up. *Couplet.*—"My friend! go on; with all thou hast, purchase an attached friend, and do not sell him for any thing." So the tortoise, taking the scorpion on her back, cast her bosom on the water, set off. In the midst of her swimming, a sound reached the ears of the tortoise, and she perceived a tapping made by some action of the scorpion: She said, what noise is this, I hear, and what is the work that you seem so busy about? The scorpion gave answer, I am only trying the point of my sting on your armour and helmet. The tortoise was incensed, and said, Unfeeling wretch! for you I have cast my life into a whirlpool of dangers; and you are passing the water by the help of the boat of my back; if you don't make gratitude an obligation, if you set no weight upon the rights of early intercourse, what at least is the reason of stinging? since it is certain that no harm can come to me from this act; nor will your heart-tearing sting have the least effect on my back, resembling a marble quarry. *Couplet.*—" It is most probable, that he will wound his hand and his mind; he who in violence knocks his fist against the wall." The scorpion said, God forbid that such sentiments as these should at any time of my life, pass through my mind; or should ever have entered it. It is nothing more than this, that my nature impels me to use my sting; whether the wound be on the back of a friend, or the bosom of a foe. *Verses.*—" To whomsoever there is a vicious habit, without design it will break forth from him: the scorpion will strike his sting upon a stone, although he has no power over it."

The tortoise thought with herself thus: philosophers have said truly, that to cherish a base character, is to give one's own honour to the winds, and to lose the clue of one's own affairs. *Couplet.*—" To cast gold and jewels into the dirt, is not to be regretted; to shew favour and generosity to the worthless, may be matter of regret." It is a saying of the ancients, that every one who has no nobility in his descent, hope has no portion in him; for it is unlawful to a corrupt offspring, that he should depart from the world, and not have done evil towards the society which had shown kindness toward him. *Fragment.*—" What way is it possible to educate one, vile in origin? Why should a man bring up a snake in his house? Colocynth, by cultivation, will not yield the food of the sugar-cane. That man will never gather roses, who entirely cultivates thorns." And upon the recital of these words, it must have crossed the brilliant mind of the king, that he ought to be apprehensive of the want of descent in Shanzabah, and of his baseness of caste. And it behoves him to listen, with the ear of prudence, to the advice of his affectionate servants: for he who does not pay attention to the words of his advisers, although they speak harshly and without courtesy,—the results of his proceedings, and the conclusions of his enterprises will not be clear of remorse and blame; like a sick man, who looks with an eye of contempt upon the order of the physician, and takes meat and drink according to his inclination,—most certainly, languor and debility will every moment obtain greater power over him. *Couplet.*—" If he who gives advice has spoken from a motive of severity, what harm is there? Patience is bitter, but it bears sweet fruit."

And it is to be observed, that the weakest of princes is one, who is negligent of the consequences of affairs, and who despises the business of the kingdom; who, whenever any great event falls out, lays aside caution and circumspection; and who, after the opportunity is lost, and when the enemy is become successful, casts suspicion upon his own immediate servants, and transfers the matter to any one of them. *Quatrain.*—" The thought, which it behoves thee to take in thine own affairs; wherefore shouldst thou leave it to another: and at a time, when in this manner, thou hast made a mistake; why should it be thrown upon the neck of others."

The lion said, Thou hast spoken words, right harsh; and hast transgressed beyond the bounds of respect, yet the words of one who gives advice are not to be rejected for harshness, upon the supposition that Shanzabah is my enemy, it is clear, what work he can do, and that according to events is food for me: for the source of all his activity has taken its existence from vegetables; while the support of my strength is derived from flesh; and vegetable parts are always subdued by the animal. Nor do I make that degree of account of him, that the notion of resisting me should pass through his mind, or the mad idea of fighting with me should have settled in his dark thoughts. *Couplet.*—"When shall it occur to an opponent to boast of contending with one like me? When shall a gnat be able to match against a raging elephant?"

And if Shanzabah, like the moon, should pretend to a comparison with the sun of my prosperity, which shines from the horizon of divine bounty, he will appear diminished and deficient: if, like the sun, he draws the sword against the crescent on my imperial canopy, like the royal eagle, and which is a pattern of the canopy of heaven, in the end he will sink. *Verses.*—"The empty-handed, if he plays the rich man, is like a lame horse, which acts the part of one fit for the road: I have made that animal to bear his head so high; I will again throw the noose upon his neck."

Damanah said, The king should not be deluded by what he says, that he is my food, or, I can get the better of him: for if he is not able by his own nature to contend with you, he may advance his scheme by the assistance of a party of friends; or else by fraud, hypocrisy, tales, and treachery, he may excite impressions. And I am afraid of this; that, when he has given the animals a desire of enmity to the king, (may it never be) they may breathe concord with him; for a single person, however powerful and strong in body, will not succeed against a multitude. *Fragment.*—"Gnats, when they are numerous, will assault an elephant, with all the valour and fierceness which belong to him: the little ants, when unanimous, will tear off the skin from the raging lion."

The lion said, Thy words have taken root in my heart, and I have perceived the sincerity of thy counsels; but then this idea clings to me, that I have raised him;

I raised the standard of his strength and advancement, I have spoken his praises in meetings and assemblies, I have made the recital of his prudence and honesty, sincerity and integrity, to run over my tongue; if, now, I admit the reverse of all this, I shall be characterized for breaking my word, levity of disposition, and weakness of judgment; and my words will be in abomination in all hearts, and my promise without value in all minds. *Couplet.*—" Any head, which thou thyself dost elevate, as long as thou art able, thou shalt not cast down from its place."

Damanah said, A sound judgment, and a wise plan, is this, that as soon as enmity is evinced by a friend, or the pride of lordship is observed in a servant, men should instantly bring their affairs into order, and gather up the skirt from intimacy and society with such persons; and before the enemy finds time for breakfast, they should make ready a supper for him. Although teeth are very early companions of a man, and a variety of advantages and benefits result to him from them, yet when one begins to ache, he cannot get relief from the pain but by pulling it out; and food, which replaces what is dissipated, and is the support of the material of life, when it becomes corrupt in the bowels, one cannot get free of the mischief except by expelling it. *Couplet.*—" The man, by whom thy sorrow-stricken heart is not gladdened; if truly he be like thy soul, give him up."

These whisperings of Damanah had their effect upon the lion, and he said, I am disgusted with the society of Shanzabah; and any further interview of me with him is of the number of impossibilities: this is the very best thing, that I should send some one to him, and make the whole state of the case clear, and give him leave to go wherever he likes. Damanah was afraid that if these words should reach Shanzabah, he would instantly make his innocency and gratitude clear; and that his own deceit and stratagem would come forth from the private chamber of secrecy, to the area of manifestation; so he said, O king! this way is far from caution; and so long as a word has not been spoken, room for circumspection is still left; but after it has been published, the remedy is beyond the limits of our power. *Couplet.*—"The word, whilst thou hast not spoken it, thou hast the power to speak; but thou canst not again conceal the word which has once been spoken."

The word which has passed the lips, and the arrow that has left the bow, neither will that come again within our power, nor this return to the aiming point; and it occurs among proverbs, that whatever comes to the tongue goes to waste. And one of the ancients has said, the tongue is the interpreter of the heart; the heart is the lord of the dominion of the body; and language is the spreader forth of the jewels of the treasury of existence: so long as the door of the casket of speech is closed with the fastening of silence; and the seal of silence is fixed upon the top of the casket of discourse; all the sweet herbs of peace will grow in the garden of existence, and the shrub of life will yield all the fruits of security and repose; but when the rose bush of eloquence expands its smiling leaves, and the nightingale of oratory begins to warble, no one can be safe; for the odours of the garden of discourse will be a means to refresh the heart and strengthen the brain, or the cause of defluxion of the juices of the brain, and bring on a headache; for tongues which were bound, have, by one fascinating piece of wit, loosened many difficult knots; but words, producing mischief, have, by one untimely hint, bound the neck of the speaker in heavy bonds. *Fragment.*—"If you will look with an eye of discretion upon speech, it is a stock in trade, which produces both profit and loss: and the proof to be given is this, that a witty thing, not said before, may distress a man by vexation of heart, or give him life; but it is often that the ambush of a word gives the speaker to the winds, in the moment that he brings it to his tongue."

O king! if these words should reach Shanzabah, and he should discover the nature of his situation; and he shall clearly perceive his degradation, it is possible that he may venture upon haughtiness, and begin to fight, or cause strife. Men of caution have not deemed secret punishment suitable to an open offence; nor approved of public punishment for secret crimes: the safest way is to follow up his concealed offences, with private chastisement. The lion replied, To remove or to banish my nearest friends, upon a bare suspicion, and to destroy all their claims, without any appearance of certainty, would be, with my own hands to strike a hatchet on my own foot; it would be to wander on a sudden from the path of generosity, and from the highway of integrity. *Fragment.* —" It would not be agreeable to law or reason, that the king should give a commandment without full proof, for his edict is like a decree of destiny; sometimes it takes away life, and sometimes gives it."

There is no better evidence to men possessed of authority, than their own sagacity. When this deceitful traitor shall appear, let the king regard him with a look of penetration; for the baseness of his principles will be evident in a disagreeable aspect; and the vileness of his intentions in an angry countenance: and a sure sign of the crookedness of his mind is this, that he will advance, changing colour, and agitated; and will look about, right and left, before and behind; and that he will have made ready for battle, and will have gathered himself up for resistance. The lion said, Thou sayest truly; and if anything of these signs should happen to be observed, then certainly, the dust of doubt will be removed from the path of conviction; and the unsteadiness of suspicion will be changed for a ground of certainty.

When Damanah felt that, by his strife-making breath,

the fire of evil had begun to blaze on the other side, he wanted to go and see the ox, that on his part, too, he might kindle the fire of mischief. *Couplet.*—" A quarrel between two people is like fire; an ill-disposed talebearer is one who brings the fuel." He considered that his seeing Shanzabah, ought still to be by the order and with the advice of the lion; that he might keep clear of all evil surmise. So he said, O king! if the sublime command should find the honour of promulgation, I may as well see Shanzabah; and having ascertained something of the hidden things of his mind, and the stores of his heart, I will report it. The lion gave him leave; and, like one struck by sorrow, and fallen into misfortune, went unto Shanzabah, and fulfilled all the conditions of respect and courtesy. Shanzabah, too, displaying that reverence which was suitable to the occasion, began great civility and flattery, and said, O Damanah! *Verses.*—" Bear in mind, that remembrance of me does not occur to thee. It is many days that thou hast not enlightened the sight of thy friends with the rays of thy beauty; nor hast converted the cottage of the friends into a flower garden, with the blossoms of the shrubs of endearment and society." *Couplet.*—" For ages thou dost not one moment remember that friend; who is unable for an instant not to think of thee?"

Damanah replied, If in outward appearance I have been deprived of the honour of visiting you; yet in soul and spirit I have perpetually kept company with the imagination of thy heart-expanding beauty; and have constantly been sowing the seed of love and affection in the ground of my heart. *Couplet.*—" I have pierced windows from my heart to my soul; unknown to thee, I have used many blandishments with thee."

And in the cell of retirement, and the corner of solitude, I have been engaged in the daily duties of prayers and prayers, such as may be the cause of an increase of prosperity and happiness ; and so shall it ever be. The ox said, What is the reason of such retirement ? Damanah replied, When a man cannot be master of his own will, but is captive to the authority of another ; when he cannot draw a single respiration without fear and dread ; when one moment does not pass, that a man is not fearing and trembling about his soul and body ; and a single word cannot escape him without alarm and terror; why should he not choose the corner of his hut and close the door of retirement in the face of friends and strangers ? *Quatrain.* —" From the strife of this mischief-making age, arise, and flee, wherever thou canst ; and if thou hast not a foot of flight, at least, put forth the hand, and cling to the mantle of solitude. The ox said, O Damanah ! set forth language more clear than this ; and relate the details of this concise remark, that the benefits of thy advice may be more general, and the advantage of thy discourse more complete. Damanah said, There are six things in this world, which are not possible without six other things: viz. worldly wealth, without pride and subserviency ; lust, without difficulty ; intercourse with women, without calamity ; a desire for indulgence, without disgrace ; fellowship with the wicked, without remorse ; and the service of a king, without misfortune. They never give any one a draught from the wine-cellar of the world, that he does not get intoxicated and audacious ; and that he does not raise the head of sin from the collar of haughtiness, and pride ; a man does not move a step in pursuit of lust, that he does not fall into an occasion of destruction, and no man can associate with women, that he is not overcome by all sorts of contention; no person can take up intercourse with vicious people, who make disturbances, that in the end of the matter shame does not produce its fruits; nor does any one fix his expectations on the low and base, that he does not become vile and worthless: and no man ever sought the society of a king, that he ever escaped in safety from that voracious pathless desert. *Verses.*—" The society of a king, upon grounds of analogy, consider like an ocean without a shore; to such an ocean, full of fear and danger, he who is nearest is most wretched." And upon this subject, they have said, *Couplet.*—" There are countless gains in the sea: but if you wish for peace, it is on shore."

Shanzabah said, Your words afford a demonstration of this, that something offensive on the part of the lion has befallen you; and that some fear and dread of his terribleness has overwhelmed you. Damanah replied, I do not say these things so much out of regard to myself; and am not melancholy for my own sake; but rather give greater weight, in this matter, to the part of my friends, than to my own part: for all this grief and dejection which have overcome me, is for thee: thou knowest the early ties of unanimity, the former bonds of affection between me and thee, of what kind they have been; and those vows and promises which, at the first, we made, most of them have at this end finished in fulfilment; and I have no alternative but this, to have the honour of reporting whatever may have occurred of good and evil, of advantage or injury. Shanzabah trembled all over, and said, My kind ally and affectionate friend, make me quickly acquainted with the truth of the case; and do not neglect any article of the minute points of attachment and sincerity. Damanah said, I have heard from one to be relied upon, that the lion has made it flow over his august tongue, that Shanzabah is got excessively fat, and there is not the least occasion for him at this court; his loss and his presence are on an equality; I will make an entertainment for the beasts with his flesh; and in one day, I will prepare of his body a private meal, and a public banquet. When I heard these words, as I have observed his impetuosity and arrogance, I came here, that having given you warning, I may confirm my promise by a proof; and that

I may discharge whatever in the law of manly feeling, or in the rules of honour and generosity, may be incumbent on me. *Couplet.*—"I will relate to thee all that belongs to the conditions of strict duty; take thou either advice from my words, or take thou offence." At present, the expediency of the time, I find to be in this; that thou consider of some plan; that thou set thy face with all celerity to some remedy, and draw out the business to some length. Perhaps by a stratagem, escape from this labyrinth may present itself; and that by a refinement, deliverance from this pit of destruction may give you help.

When Shanzabah heard the words of Damanah, and revolved in his mind the vows and engagements of the lion, he said, It is impossible, Damanah, that the lion should show jealousy towards me; whilst on my part no treason has appeared; and the foot of my constancy has never slipped from the road of good services: and yet, as regards thy words, too, I have a belief of their truth, and an opinion of their good meaning. It is most probable that they have spread many falsehoods against me, and have led him to this stage of anger by artifice and deceit: for there is a worthless party in his service, each an illustrious master in telling tales, saucy and insolent in treachery and violence: and these men he has often tried, and observed the variety of their treacheries and wicked doings; and therefore, whatever of the same sort he hears with respect to others, he believes it, and applies analogy to it: for of a truth, by the contagion of the society of the wicked, evil thoughts arise with regard to the virtuous; and by this wrong opinion, the path of right is concealed. The fate of the duck, and his error of experience, is sufficient evidence to this effect, and is a full direction to this state of things.

Damanah enquired what that might be? and Shanzabah told this

STORY.

A duck saw the light of the moon in the water, and thought it was a fish; he aimed at it, to seize it, but got nothing, and in this manner he several times made the experiment; and when he saw that his profit by that sport was the same as the profit of a thirsty man who looks at the vapour of the desert, or the gains of poor men thinking of treasures, from searching through desolate habitations, he entirely abandoned the pursuit of fish, and all at once neglected his proper occupation. On the following night, whenever he saw a fish he thought it was the brightness of the moon, and would not attack it, nor be in any way mindful of it; but would say. *Verse.*—"He who tries what has been tried, confusion will surround him." So the fruit of his experience was this; that he used to be always hungry, and to pass his days without food and sustenance. And if they have made the lion listen to any thing about me, by the rule, that he who listens is alienated, some disgust will have arisen in his mind, and he will have held it for true; and his motive will have been his very experience of others: while the fact is, that from me to others, there is as much difference, as from brilliant day to dark night, from the lofty dome to the low centre. *Couplets.*—"Do not judge the case of the virtuous from thyself; although, in writing, lion and milk are the same: both kinds of flies eat from the same place; from the one came a sting, from the other honey: both kinds of deer feed on the same grass and water; from the one comes blood, and from the other pure musk."

Damanah said, Perhaps the aversion of the lion may not be from this cause, but rather from this, that it is a habit with princes, that, without any just claim, they will distinguish one man by high advancement, and another who is one of just pretensions, they will make an object of ruin and plunder. *Verses.*—"The king of Hoomūz never saw me, and without a word did me a hundred favours: the king of Yazd saw me, I repeated his praise, and he gave me nothing: Such is the practice of kings. Thou, O Hafiz, fret not; may the Lord, who sends food to all, give them their help and assistance."

Shanzabah said, If this aversion, which you reported to me of the lion, is without cause, then by no help can the foot of steadfastness measure the road of stability, nor can the eye of hope behold the countenance of our desires; for if there be any motive for anger, one can obviate it by pacifying or apologizing; but if, God protect us! there be no motive for it, or if by imposture and calumny they have given a change to his temper, remedy will fall short of it, and the thought of providing against it be insufficient; since there is no apparent measure to falsehood and slander, nor any certain limit to deceit and fraud. Now, in all that has occurred between me and the lion, I do not perceive any offence in myself, except this; that in judgment and deliberation, on some points, even for his advantage, I have differed from him; and in preparing and advancing his designs, I may occasionally, according to the exigency of the time, have said something not suitable to his pleasure: he may, perhaps, have charged this to boldness and disrespect, and have reckoned it as a species of audacity and saucy familiarity; yet not one of these things which have proceeded from me, has been devoid of general advantage; and with all this, shewing a regard for his dignity and awfulness, I have not upon the whole shown any insolence, but have fulfilled all the conditions of reverence and deep respect: so, how can it possibly be supposed that affectionate advice can be a cause of alarm; or faithful services become a motive to enmity. *Couplet.*—" Medicine has been a cause of illness, so here what hope is there of the disorder passing away, or of the health of the sick man ?" And if it be not also this, it is possible that the pride of power, and the independent feeling of dominion, may have been the inducement with him to be offended with me; for it is a requisite of haughtiness, and the demand of greatness, that they are naturally averse to those who give them advice, and give honour, by their confidence, to the treacherous and to flatterers. And hence it is, that the learned have said, to dive with a crocodile to the bottom of the river, or to suck drops of poison from the lips of a snake whose tail is cut off, is nearer to safety than the service of a king; and is better and much more for safety and quiet than advancement with princes. I had learnt that the perils of serving kings are many, and that the evils of engaging in their affairs are countless. And some of the masters of philosophy have compared kings to fire; for though a ray of favour may give light to the dark cottage of those who live on hopes, yet by the flame of punishment he also consumes the granary of the ancient claims of his servants: and sound prudence agrees to this, that whoever is nearest to the fire, his injury is the greatest. While that class who, from a distance, enjoying the sight of this fire, are ignorant of its conflagration, have a fancy of some great delight, and a notion of some great advantages in obtaining a near approach to monarchs; while in truth it is not at all so: for if they should get a right apprehension of princely severity, and of royal dread and awe, it would be clear to them that a thousand years of favour are not equal to one hour of punishment. And a corroboration of this, is the tale of the dispute between the hawk and the domestic fowl.

Damanah desiring to hear it, Shanzabah related this

STORY.

A sporting hawk once fell into an argument with a domestic fowl, and beginning a contest with her, said, Thou art a most faithless and false bird: whilst the inscription on the page of good morals is fidelity; although fidelity, by the purport of this passage—verily, the perfection of a promise is a part of the faith—is a proof of perfection in religion. And generosity and manly virtue also require that a man should not inscribe the page of his fortune with the character of infidelity. *Couplet.*—"The dog, in whom there is gratitude for a bit of roast meat, is better than that man in whom there is no gratitude." The hen replied, What ingratitude hast thou seen in me; and what breach of duty hast thou observed? The hawk said, The sign of thy ingratitude is this, that, together with all this, that men shew so much indulgence in thy behalf; and that without any trouble or exertions of thine, they provide water and corn, from which the material of life receives support; that, day and night, being well aware of thy condition, they persevere in guarding and watching thee; and that by their power thou hast thy board and lodging; yet whenever they are inclined to catch thee, fleeing before and behind them, thou goest flying from roof to roof, and running from corner to corner. *Couplet.*—"Thou dost not acknowledge the rights of salt; and art frightened at thy benefactor."

Whilst I, although I be a wild animal, if I form an attachment, tho' for two or three days, and eat my food from their hand, attentive to the claims of this, I pursue the game, and give it to them; and how far soever I may have gone, at the slightest sound that I hear, I come flying back. *Couplet.*—"The bird that is taught on the hand, how far soever they may throw him, comes back with joyful wing, as soon as they say, come here."

The hen answered, Thou sayest right. Thy coming back, and my running away, are from this; that thou hast never seen a hawk roasted on a spit; but I have seen many a fowl broiling on a pan. If thou too hadst seen this, certainly thou wouldest not hover about them; but while I flee from roof to roof, thou wouldest be fleeing from hill to hill. And I have produced this example for this, that thou mayest know, that the class, who seek the society of kings, have no knowledge of their severity; for whoever has seen the effects of their severity, has neither any knowledge of tranquility nor any impression of repose. *Couplet.*—" To those who are nearest, there is the greatest consternation; for they comprehend royal severity."

To which Damanah replied, It is not likely that the lion should, because of his imperial grandeur, his pomp and good fortune, make such reflections with regard to thee; for thou hast many talents, and innumerable accomplishments; and princes are not at any time above the want of persons of talent. Shanzabah said, Perhaps my talents may have been the cause of his aversion: for to a horse of swift paces, his talent becomes a cause of ill usage; and to a fruitful tree, because of its fruit, the head and branches are broken; the nightingale, for his very talent, is confined, in the prison of a cage; and the peacock, for his elegance and beauty, is plucked of his wings and feathers, and disgraced. *Fragment.*—" All my knowledge is become a calamity to me; like his fur to the fox, and his feathers to the peacock; my talents are become my faults; or else to my head, not of dust, but of gems would have been the diadem."

And to be sure, since men without merit are more numerous than people of merit, and that an inherent animosity exists between them; getting advantage by their number, they go to such lengths in degrading the position of the meritorious, that setting forth all their doings, active and passive, in the garb of offence, they represent integrity in the shape of treachery, and honesty in the dress of baseness: and they convert that very merit, which is a cause of prosperity, and a means of happiness, into a matter of misery and a means of disgrace. *Couplet.*— "The eye of the malevolent, may it be plucked out; merit appears a defect in his sight." And an eminent man has said, on this subject. *Couplets.*—" If any virtue bursts out in the midst, some worthless fellow lays his vile hand upon it; they bring the affairs of a virtuous man to ruin, while they bring his virtues into contempt." And they have said, in describing the injustice of those who look out for faults. *Verses.*—" The eye of equity, when it is clear-sighted, counts pearls when they are but glass beads; the practice of great men, is equity of conduct; but the practice of the mean is nothing but biting and scratching; and he who has not a heart susceptible of pity, casts an imputation of *woollen* upon *silk.*"

Damanah said, It is possible that evil-minded persons may have made this attempt; according to that disposition of fate, what may be the course of your conduct? Shanzabah said, If my destiny be not in accordance with it, no injury whatever will come from it, into the limits of existence. But if the Divine decree, and the predestination of God shall shew conformity with their fraud and deceit, it will not be possible nor within my power to avert it by any stratagem. *Verse.*—" When destiny goes before, of what avail is contrivance?"

Damanah said, A prudent man ought, in all circumstances, to make extensive forethought the forerunner of his proceedings; for no man ever laid the foundation of his conduct upon prudence, who did not obtain success over his desires. Shanzabah answered thus, Prudence may be of use, when fate shall not have made a decree to the contrary of it; and stratagem will produce advantage, at a time when fate does not run in opposition to it: but while there exists an ordinance of destiny, neither remedy helps, nor stratagem yields advantage; escape from the fetters of fate or the prison of destiny, by stratagem and contrivance, is not to be contemplated by any man. *Couplet.*—" That fire, which the hand of fate kindled, burnt up every thought and plan."

And when the great and glorious creator shall bring any decree, with the probe of carelessness, He makes the sight of the vigilant dark and confused; so that the way of escape from that decree becomes hidden before them:

"when fate comes, perception is blinded." *Couplet.*—"At the moment of the execution of fate and destiny, they make the cunning blind and deaf." But perhaps thou hast never heard the story of the villager and the nightingale, and their disputation. So, at the desire of Damanah, he related the

STORY.

They have related, that a villager had a garden, sweet and joyful; and a field of flowers, fresher than the rose-beds of Iram; the air of it might give due temperature to the breezes of spring, and the odour of its exhilirating herbs would perfume the brain of the soul. *Verses.*—"It was a bed of roses, like the flower garden of youth; a field of flowers, well-watered with the water of life; the notes of its nightingales exciting enjoyment, and its gales spreading odours, bringing repose."

And in one corner of the plantation there was a rose-bush, fresher than the shrub of prosperity; more splendid than the branches of the tree of enjoyment. Every morning there used to blossom on it a flower, painted like the cheeks of heart-alluring damsels of delicate minds, or the complexion of jasmine-bosomed, lily-scented maids; and the gardener, falling into raptures with that beautiful flower, would exclaim, *Couplet.*—"I know not what the rose whispers, but between her lips, that she brings the silent nightingale again into lamentation."

The gardener, coming one day, according to his established custom, to amuse himself with the rose, saw a nightingale complaining, who was rubbing his face among the leaves of the rose, and with his sharp bill was tearing to bits the sewing of its golden binding. *Couplet.*—"The nightingale, if he looks upon the rose, grows intoxicated; and the end of the clue of free will goes from his hand."

The gardener, observing the dispersion of the leaves of the rose, rent the collar of patience with the hand of agitation, and hung the mantle of his heart upon the soul-piercing thorns of uneasiness. Next day the same circumstance took place; and the flame of separation from the flower. *Verse.*—"Laid another scar upon his former scar. And on the third day again, by the work of the beak of the bird." *Verse.*—"The flower was plundered, but the thorn was left."

This affliction being excited by the nightingale in the heart of the villager, he laid the snare of deception in his way, caught him with the grain of stratagem, and confined him in the prison of a cage. The heartless nightingale opened his mouth, like a parrot, and said, Worthy sir, for what reason hast thou confined me? for what cause art thou inclined to punish me? If thou hast formed this plan for the sake of hearing my songs, truly my nest is in thy garden; and every morning my music gallery is on all sides of the rose-beds. But if thou hast allowed any other purpose to pass through thy fancy, give me information of what is in thy mind. The gardener said, *Couplet.*—"How long wilt thou vex me? O Lord! mayest thou no longer live, O rival; how long wilt thou conceal her face? O Lord! mayest thou be removed, O veil." Dost thou at all know what thou hast done to my fortune, and how frequently thou hast distressed me by a separation from my lovely friends; the just return for such conduct, in the way of retribution, may be exactly this,—that thou art left separated from friends and country, art parted from enjoyment and pleasure, and dost weep in the corner of a prison; for I also am oppressed with separation, and am lamenting in the hut of sorrow. *Couplet.*—"Weep, O nightingale, if there is to thee, with me, any thought of love; for we are two afflicted lovers, and our business is grief."

The nightingale said, Depart from this thought, and reflect, if I for this extent of crime, that I have torn a rose, am become a prisoner, thou, who dost tear a heart, what thy state shall be. *Verses.*—"The revolving sphere, upon principles of analogy, is over mindful of right: whoever does good, the same befals him; and if he has done evil, mischief will reach him."

These words were effectual on the mind of the villager, and he liberated the nightingale. The bird then loosening his tongue in freedom, said, Since thou hast done a kindness to me, certainly, in obedience to "is there then any recompence for generosity, except generosity?" Some compensation must be made: know that under the earth of the tree, where thou art standing, there is a dish full of gold; take it up, and make use of it in thy wants. The villager dug up the place, and found the words of the nightingale correct. He said, It is a wonder, O nightingale, that thou seest a dish beneath the earth, and didst not perceive the snare under the dust. The nightingale replied, Thou hast not learnt that "when destiny alights, caution is vain." *Verse.*—"No one can contend against what is ordained. When a divine decree receives the dignity of descent, neither light remains to the eye of perception, nor do contrivance and prudence produce advantage." *Verses.*—"Twist not back, with the fist, the hand of fate, for hand has no power for any thing; caution is of no avail against destiny; whatever proceeds from fate, approve of that."

Which fable I have related for this purpose, that it may be understood that I am no match for the hand of destiny and fate; nor have I any remedy but to lay the head of resignation on the line of the divine commandment. *Couplet.*—"The end of all my attachment is the threshold of the Lord, who loves me; for all that passes over my head, is his design."

Damanah rejoined, Shanzabah, all that I have learnt of a certainty, or have definitely understood, is this, that whatever the lion may have imagined about thee, is neither because of the calumny of enemies, nor the abundance of thy merits, nor the ill-temper of kings; but it is rather the height of treachery and falsehood, which has impelled him to it; for he is a prosperous tyrant, an ill-tempered deceiver, and a hypocrite; the beginning of his acquaintance bestow the sweetness of life; but the conclusions of his service have the bitterness of death. You should form to yourself the idea, that he is a painted venomous snake; his exterior adorned with many spots of various colours; and his interior, provided with deadly poison, against which no antidote is beneficial. *Couplet.*—"He is all fraud, hypocrisy, cunning, and delusion; neither honesty nor honour—neither patience nor forbearance."

Shanzabah said, I have tasted the food of the honey of favour; now is the season for the wound of the sting: a long period I have passed in pleasure and ease—now is the time for the assault of trouble and sorrow. *Couplet.*—"My heart, for a while, thou didst taste the flavour of union; now thou must see the grief of separation."

And in truth it is the angel of death which seized me by the collar, and brought me into this wilderness; for otherwise, how was I suitable to society with the lion? A person who feeds upon me, and to whom I am food; it must have been, that, with a thousand snares, he would not be able to draw me towards him, nor to throw me, by a hundred thousand stratagems, into the trap of his familiarity. *Couplet.*—"Who am I, that the good fortune of a union with him should be my ambition? This, that I still behold him at a distance, is it not enough for me?"

But the divine determination, and the flattering voice of Damanah, have cast me into this pathless desert of destruction: and now the hand of management falls short of the skirt of remedy; and the course of my purposes, because of the neglect of prudence aforethought, is not according to my heart's desire: and I, by reason of vain wishes and corrupt fancies, have kindled such a fire as this for myself; and whilst the smoke has not yet come before me, I am burnt with the flame of grief, and the heat of melancholy? *Verse.*—"How shall I act? I have done it myself. What remedy is there for one's own deeds?" And the ancients have said, Whosoever is not content with a bare competency of worldly riches, but pursues a superfluity, is a likeness of that person who arrives at a hill of diamonds, and his sight falls each moment on a larger piece; and forming a notion of the vastness of its price, he goes forwards till he reaches the place, where the object of search falls into his hands: but then his return will be impracticable, because the broken pieces of the diamonds will have cut and scratched his feet; but that forgetful man, being absorbed in the thought of covetousness, has no knowledge of the circumstance; and therefore, in the utmost regret, coming to destruction on that mountain, he takes up his abode in the stomach of the birds. *Couplet.*—"From excess of pursuit, thy affairs are brought to ruin; if thou desirest profit, seek not excess beyond due measure."

Damanah observed, Thou hast here said words, very much to be admired; for every calamity which befals a man, the source of it will be avarice and desire. *Couplet.* "Depart from coveting, for it is an affliction to the soul and the heart: he who covets is, in all places, and by all people, despised."

The neck that is bound in the chain of covetousness, is ultimately cut through by the sword of disgrace; and the head, in which the folly of avarice has fixed itself, in the end, will be rubbed in the dust of ignominy. There is many a man, who from excess of covetousness and avarice, with the hope of prosperity, has fallen into the trackless wilds of misery; and upon the scent of gain, has been caught in a disastrous place of injury: just as the huntsman had a desire to seize the skin of the fox, and the paw of the leopard tore the life out of his body.

Shanzabah asked how that happened, and Damanah said,—

STORY.

A huntsman was passing one day through the desert, he saw a fox, extremely brisk and active, who was roaming about in the open space of the plain, and playing his tricks, was exhibiting himself on every side. His skin being pleasing to the huntsman, he formed the idea of selling it for a great price; and his covetous faculty set him upon this, that keeping upon the traces of the fox, he found out his hole. So digging a pit near the hole, and covering it with sticks and rubbish, he laid out a dead animal on the top of it, and sitting down in ambush, he kept waiting for the capture of the fox. It chanced that the fox came out of his hole, and the scent of the carcase attracting him, gradually led him to the edge of the pit. He said to himself, although by the smell of this carcase, the brain of desire is perfumed, yet an odour of danger also comes to the palate of caution: and the wise have never exposed themselves to an affair, which may bear a probability of danger, nor have entered upon an undertaking, in which the possibility of mischief is to be anticipated. *Couplet.*—"Wheresoever they draw a line of difficulty, take pains to keep without line."

And though it be possible that some dead animal may be here, yet this is also possible, that they may have arranged some snare beneath it; and at all events caution is best. *Fragment.*—"When two affairs present themselves to thee, that thou canst not tell which ought to be done, that in which there is a supposition of danger, that must be made unlawful to thee; and that which may be without fear and danger, upon that exactly thou shouldst be stedfast."

So the fox, making these reflections, went off from the thought of that meat, and followed the path of safety. In the meantime, a hungry leopard, came down from the mountain, and at the smell of the dead body flung himself on the pit. The huntsman, when he heard the noise of the trap, and the sound of the fall of the animal, imagined it to be the fox. In the excess of covetousness, without the least deliberation, he threw himself after him; and the leopard, under the notion that he would prevent him from eating the body, jumped up, and tore open his belly. The greedy huntsman, by the baseness of avarice, fell into the snare of destruction; and the abstemious fox, by casting off covetousness, found escape from the labyrinth of misfortune. And the use of the fable is this, that the evil of covetousness, and the trouble of excess in pursuit of gain, will make a free man a slave, and a slave more abject. *Couplet.*—"If thou couldest gain one lock of hair, beyond what belongs to thy head; by the dust of the feet of the holy, it would give a head ache."

Shanzabah said, I committed an error; that, at first, I chose the service of the lion, and did not consider that he does not know the value of services. For they have said, that to associate with a person who does not acknowledge the worth of it, or to serve any one who does not know the value of it, is parallel to this; that a man, in hopes of a crop, should scatter seed in a salt land, or whisper about his sorrows and his joys, into the ear of one deaf when his mother bore him, or write fresh and lively odes on the surface of running water, make love to the pictures in a bath, or hope for a shower of rain from the dust of a whirlwind. *Fragment.*—"To expect constancy in a king, would be much the same, as to look for fruit, on the branches of the black cypress: a plant of the willow will not yield thee the sugar of the cane, although thou give it, a thousand times, water from the river of immortality."

Damanah said, Have done with such words, and pursue the remedy for thy affairs. Shanzabah replied,

What help can I call forth, what device can I bring forward? For I have learnt all the moral qualities of the lion; and my own sagacity comes to this conclusion, that the lion wishes nothing but what is good and well, with respect to me; but his intimate adherents are labouring in my ruin, and are making great exertions for my downfal. And if it be so, the turn of the beam of the balance of my life inclines more to the scale of extinction, than to the scale of continuance: for treacherous oppressors, and deceitful tyrants, when, setting their backs together, they join hand in hand, and with one accord make an attack on any one, in every case they cast him down, just as the wolf, the raven, and the jackall, formed a design against the camel; and, by acting together, overcame him, and attained their object and their wishes.

Damanah asked how that was?

STORY.

They have related that a black-eyed raven, a sharp clawed wolf, and a jackall full of deceit, were in the service of a hunting lion; and their forest was near the public high road. The camel of a certain merchant had sunk down in that neighbourhood, and after some time, picking up strength, went about, on every side, seeking for pasture. His way fell across the forest; and when he came near the lion, he saw no alternative but service and reverence. The lion, too, bestowing caresses on him, enquired into the particulars of his fortune; and after receiving information about that, put some questions about his abode and occupation. *Couplet.*—"Hitherto, if I have had any free will in my conduct; when I beheld thee the reins of free will fell into my hand."

Whatsoever your majesty may ordain will, no doubt, involve the good of your servants. *Verse.*—"Thou knowest what is good for us, better than we do." The lion said, If thou hast any desire, remain happy and safe in my society. The camel was delighted, and passed his time in the forest; and so, when a long time had passed, he became extremely fat.

One day the lion had gone out in search of game; and a raging elephant falling in with him, a stout battle and a fierce conflict took place between them; several wounds befalling the lion, he came back to the forest, yelling aud lacerated; and lay down in a corner. The wolf, the raven, and the jackall, who by thrusting themselves in used to pick their bits from the table of his bounty, were left without means of support; and so, from the natural generosity of the lion, and from that simple kindness which princes have for their servants and officers, when he saw them in that condition, he was affected, and said, your troubles be harder upon me than my own pains; if you can get hold of any head of game in this vicinity, I will go out, and having settled the business for you, will come back. So they, leaving the presence of the lion went into a corner, introducing the path of consultation between them, they said, What is the good to us of this camel's staying in this forest? there is neither any advantage to the king from him, nor have we any attachment to him; we ought to put the lion up to crushing him; and so for two or three days the king will have rest from the search after a morsel and a bit of food; and to us also, according to our condition, some advantage will accrue. The jackall said, Do not turn yourselves about this fancy. The lion has given him security, and taken him into his service; and whoever shall give a king a desire for treachery, or encourage him to break an engagement, will have committed treason; and a traitor is, under all circumstances, shunned; and God and man are displeased with him. *Verses.*—"Every man, in whom there is any scheme of treacherousness, his religion is devoid of integrity and probity; the sterling value of a man is by his probity, and the base coin of mankind is by treachery." The raven said, We might think of some stratagem in this matter, and might extricate the lion from the obligations of his engagement: Do you watch in this place, while I go and come back again. So he came before the lion and stood still. The lion enquired, Have you traced any game? have you brought tidings of any prey? The raven answered, O king! our eyes, from hunger, will not do their office to any one of us, and the faculty of motion, too, is not left; but a method is come into my mind, to which, if the king shall give his approbation, to all of us great comfort and sufficient plenty will be obtained. The lion desired him to unfold the meaning of these words, that comprehension might fall upon the particulars of the case. The raven said, This camel is a foreigner among us, and there is not any advantage to be contemplated from him in society; he is a prey for the haste of the occasion, which is come into our hands; a head of game fallen into the snare. The lion got in a passion and said, Dust be upon the head of the fellows of this age, for they have nothing but a practice of hypocrisy and a habit of treachery; and they altogether abandon the path of kindness, liberality, and manly sentiments. *Verses.*—"In the people of this age, to whom fidelity is not dear, seek not faithfulness, for except violence, nothing is their practice; a dog is better than those dumb cats, who, with their stratagems, hunt after nothing, but around the dinner table. In what sect is a breach of promise allowed? In what religion would it be tolerated to form a design against the person, to whom yourself have given refuge? *Couplet.*—"Any strong branch which, by thee, is grown tall; do not break it by thine own hand, for that also is to break thyself."

The raven replied, I understand all these principles; but then, philosophers have said that, an individual may be made a victim for a whole house; that a household may be made a sacrifice for a whole tribe; a tribe for a whole city; and the inhabitants of a city may be sacrificed for the august person of a king who is in danger, since by his preservation a benefit may be conferred upon the inhabitants of a whole region of the earth. And besides, some clear way may be found for breaking this engagement; so that he who made the promise, may be free from the quality of treachery, and his mind be preserved from the pains of a sting, and the danger of starving. The lion hung down his head, and the raven came back and said to his friends, I have laid the case before the lion; at first he resisted, but at last he became docile. Now our plan is this: Let us all go to the camel, and give a vivid account of the hunger of the lion, and of the trouble which has befallen him; and let us say, we have passed our days in gladness under the protection of the prosperity, and in the shade of the dignity of this auspicious monarch, and to-day, when this event has occurred, honour demands this, that we make life and soul a ransom for him; or else we shall be stigmatized for ingratitude for his bounty, and shall be excluded from the distinction of honourable and generous feelings: our duty lies in this, that we go in a body to the lion, and pour forth our thanks for his bounty and gracious favour, and acknowledge that no service can arise at our hands, except this, that we make our souls and lives a ransom for him. And then let each of us say, to-day let the king make his breakfast of me; but let the others always raise some objection; and thus, perhaps, death may be fixed upon the camel.

Accordingly, they went in company to the camel, and repeated all these details to him; and because such was the simplicity of his heart, he was deluded by their wiles and cajoling; and having settled every thing exactly in the way that has been described, they all went to the lion. And when they had acquitted themselves of the declaration of their gratitude and admiration; and of the setting forth of praises and prayers for him; the raven, giving loose to his tongue, said, *Couplet.*—" O king! through the world may prosperity be thine; at the banquet of joy, may festivity be thine." Our repose is dependent upon the health of the person of the king; now, that a case of necessity has occurred, and that enough to save life may be produced to the king from my flesh, it is fit that he should condescend to kill and make use of me. Then all the others said, What is the good of eating thee? what satisfaction can there be in thy food? *Verse.*—"Who art thou, that thou shouldest ever be taken even into the account?"

The raven, when she heard these words, hung down her head; and the jackal began his speech, saying, *Couplet.*—"O mighty king! at whose hand, in the season of vengeance, the messenger of death takes the daily list of the slaughter." A long period has elapsed, that I have lived safe from the heat of the sun of vicissitudes, under the shade of thy life-increasing good fortune; this day, when the moon of the glory of this presence is overcome by the eclipse of distress, I am desirous that the star of success should take its rise from the horizon of my condition; and that the king, making me his food, may be free from anxiety about breakfast. To which the others replied, All that thou hast said, is from excess of affection, and from the essence of dutifulness; but then thy flesh is rank, coarse, and unwholesome; may it never be that by feeding on it the illness of the king should increase.

The jackal was silent; and the wolf advancing, loosened his tongue, and said, *Couplet.*—"I pray that, O king, the Lord may be thy aid; may the enemy, in the day of battle, be thy pursuit." I, too, making myself a sacrifice for the king, am anxious that his majesty, with cheerful smiles, should give my limbs a place at the roots of his teeth. His allies said, Thou hast spoken these words out of pure fidelity, and genuine attachment; but then thy flesh would produce a choking, and in mischief it might stand in the place of deadly poison.

So the wolf stepped back, and the camel, stretching out

his long neck, and tossing up the long reins of "every tall man is a fool," began his speech, and after the proper duties of prayer, said, *Couplet.*—"O great king! at whose threshhold the azure heaven has opened many gates of victory and triumph." I have been brought up in this presence, and educated under this government: if I am fit for his majesty's kitchen, or may serve for the supply of his table, there is no trouble about my life. *Couplet.*—"I will not arise from the end of thy street, so long as I have life; and if the thing extends to my life, I will depart from all care for my life."

All the rest, agreeing in words, exclaimed, These words are from excess of affection, and from holiness of attachment; and in fact, thy flesh is sweet of digestion and wholesome for the constitution of the king; blessings be upon thy resolution, that, towards thy benefactor, thou hast made no difficulty about thy life; and by this conduct thou hast left a good name for a remembrance. *Couplet.* "The resolution of a valorous man. A hundred thousand Dirhams. When the affair becomes a question of life, then is the occasion for its exercise." Then, all at once, they made an attack upon the camel; and the poor wretch could not draw a breath before they had torn his limbs in pieces.

And I have produced this example for this; that thou mayest understand that the deceit of men of selfish views, particularly when they are in union with each other, will never be without effect. Damanah said, And what defence dost thou think of against it? Shanzabah answered thus, At present, my thoughts wander from the path of sound conduct. But I know no help for it, except battle and contention, war, and slaughter; for whoever is killed in guarding his property or protecting his life, is included within the circle of martyrs; and the virtue of this saying, —"whoever is killed, except on his own account, is a martyr,"—extends to him. And besides, if my death is determined and ordained at the hand of the lion, at least let me be killed honourably; let me perish with character and dignity. *Couplet.*—"If I die with a good name, it may pass; fame must be for me, for the body is for death."

Damanah said, A prudent man does not go before hand in battle, and in time of war does not think precedence right; for "the first blow is the violence;" and to engage in great dangers, of our own free-will, is no proof of cleverness; for, indeed, men of judgment set about an affair of enmity with courtesy and conciliation, and confess that it is better to repel a quarrel by gentleness. *Verses.*—"An agreeable deception is better than disagreeable anger; it is better to scatter water than fire: that desire which may be accomplished in gentleness, why should the reins be turned towards anger? And besides, a man should not hold a weak enemy to be small and insignificant; for if he should fail of power and strength, it is likely that he may not be deficient in deceit and stratagem; and by fraud and cunning he may raise up such a fire of strife, that the flame of it will not be quenched by the water of deliberate plans; and thou thyself hast known the violence of the lion; and his irresistible power is above the want of commentary and enlargement: therefore, take full account of his enmity, and be not inattentive to the fierce assault of his fighting. For whoever holds an enemy contemptible, and does not think about the consequences of the conflict, will be disgraced; as the envoy of the ocean was by his contempt of the Tītū. And, at the request of Shanzabah, he related the

STORY.

They have related that on the shores of the Indian ocean, there is a kind of bird which they call Tītū, and a pair of them had a safe retreat on the sea coast, and had taken up their abode at the water-side. When the season of eggs was fully come, the female said, we must look out for a place to lay the eggs, where we may live in peace of mind. The male replied, here is a nice place, and a delightful spot; and to remove at present from this place seems impossible; the eggs must be laid. The female replied, here is a point for deliberation, for if the sea should raise up a wave and carry off our young, and all the labour of our life and time should be wasted, what arrangement can be made against that? The male said, I have no notion that the envoy of the ocean can exercise this audacity, or that he will shew such neglect of regard for us; and on the supposition that he should think of such irreverence, and should go so far that our little ones are drowned, justice may be obtained of him. *Couplet.*— "I will break the sphere together, if it rolls round against my wishes, I am not one, who will bear ill usage from the sphere of heaven."

The female said, To wander from our own limits, and to boast beyond our means, is unsuitable to a discreet man; by what power canst thou threaten the envoy of the ocean with thy vengeance; and with what pomp canst thou take the place of contest and conflict with him? *Couplet.*—"Thou art making a Turkish inroad for thine own devastation; thou livest as a sparrow, and wilt act the hawk." Get along from this thought, and choose, for the eggs, a safe spot, a secure place, and do not turn the head from my advice; for any one who does not listen to the words of his advisers, and does not shape his conduct according to the counsel of his affectionate friends, that will happen to him which befel the tortoise.

The male asked how that was, and the female said,

STORY.

They have related, that in a lake, whose water, by the pureness of its bosom, would, like a clear mirror, receive any reflection, and in freshness and sweetness might afford information about the fountain of life, or the springs of paradise, two ducks and a tortoise were inhabitants; and by the laws of neighbourhood, the thread of their circumstances was spun out into mutual good faith; and having the same shade, or neighbourhood, ended in having the same house; and being delighted with the sight of each other, they passed their days, for a long period, in great comfort. *Couplet.*—"Sweet is the life that is passed in the sight of our friends; sweet is the moment that passes with those who love us affectionately."

Suddenly the hand of treacherous fortune began, with the nails of vicissitude, to scratch the face of their condition; and the sphere, a looking glass in colour, began to display forms of separation in the mirror of their days. *Verse.*—"And what enjoyment is there, which fortune does not darken?" *Verses.*—"How sweet is the wine from the cup of union with those who have stolen our hearts; but there is behind it, the sick head-ache of parting: at this table, no man can bite a mouthful of bread, but a stone gets between his teeth."

A complete failure appeared in the water, which was their material of life, and their means of subsistence; and a dreadful alteration was apparent. The ducks, when they got full information of the particulars of this event, withdrew their heart from their beloved home, and fastened it on the design of emigration. *Verses.*—"Travelling is better for that man, when, in his own place, his mind is vexed with sorrow about this and that; for although the vexations of travelling are very bad, yet they are better than the sufferings of our native land." So with hearts full of grief, and eyes full of moisture, coming to the tortoise, and introducing words of parting benediction, they said, *Couplet.*—"The evil eye of the times has parted us from thee; that evil eye of the times, what can I say, for what things has it done?" The tortoise lamented about the anguish of parting, and drew forth his complaints in great sorrow, saying, What words are these? How can life be thought of without you? In what way can life be possessed without confidential friends? *Verses.*—"Oh!

without thee, existence is hateful; indeed, without thee, what is existence? For every mode of life, which must be without thee, is but a kind of death, under the name of existence." And since I have not the strength to bear this farewell, how shall I be able to endure a separation? *Couplet.*—"I am still the stately cypress, by those eyes which are not yet departed; but my heart, at the thought of your departure, is like a trembling willow."

The ducks replied,

To us also the heart is lacerated by the many thorns of separation, and in our bosoms, by the blazing of the flame of the fire of leaving thee, there is a burning beyond excess. But it is close at hand, that the difficulty of want of water should give the dust of our being to the wind of extinction; therefore, of necessity, relinquishing friends and country, we make choice of the affliction of departure. *Couplet.*—"Of his own accord, the heartless lover never left the street of his beloved; no man of his own choice, ever left the gardens of paradise."

The tortoise said,

My friends, ye know that the evil of a failure of water is greater with respect to me; and my existence, without water, would not be possible. At this time, the claims of ancient intimacy require this, that you should take me along with you, and not leave me alone in the melancholy abode of separation. *Couplet.*—"Thou art my soul, and thou hast the design of going away; when the soul departs, what can this lifeless body do?"

They said, Thou single-minded friend, and noble associate! the grief of leaving thee is greater to us, than quitting the place of our birth; sorrow at parting with thee is, to our heart, a cause of additional melancholy and depression. And we, wherever we may go, and though we may dwell in the utmost comfort, and should pass our days in complete enjoyment, yet without the sight of thee, the fountain of our joy will be dark, and the eye of our fortune, dull: for neither have we any desire, except union and intercourse with thee; but then it is extremely difficult for us to move along upon the surface of the earth, and to get through a long and tedious journey; whilst thy flight through the expanse of the air, and keeping company with us, is out of the question. Under this disposition of nature, how can there be any travelling together? By what means can we keep company?

The tortoise said, Your understanding is able to raise up some remedy, even for this matter; and a device for this purpose also may result from your thoughts; for I, with a soul distracted at the idea of your removal, and a heart broken with the burden of separation, what arrangement can I make? *Couplet.*—"In every affair, the whole heart is needed from the beginning; sound plans never come from a broken heart."

The ducks replied, Dear friend! during this period, we have perceived a little fickleness in thee, and have discovered some inconsistency and want of steadiness. Perhaps thou wilt not act upon what we shall say, and wilt not be firm in the promise that thou mayest make. The tortoise answered, How can it be that you should give an opinion for the bettering of my condition, and that I should think in opposition to it; or that I should not fulfil a promise which may be for the sake of my own benefit? *Couplet.*—"I have bound myself by a vow, that I will certainly never turn away my head from my promise; I have made it a condition, that I am not to deviate from the conditions. The ducks said, The condition then is this, that when we have lifted thee up, and are flying through the air, thou shalt absolutely not speak a single word; for every one whose eyes shall fall upon us, will throw in a word, and will utter some saying of broad hint and allusion. It is necessary that, whenever, by speech or gesture, you may hear anything, or observe any action, thou close up the path of reply; and that thou loosen not the tongue, neither for good nor bad. The tortoise said, I will obey your orders; and, positively, placing the seal of silence on my lips, I will not be exposed to answer any creature. *Fragment.*—"I came at length to an old man, in the farthest parts of Greece: I said to him, O thou, who hast wisdom and understanding, what hast thou learnt from men? which is best in all conditions? He said, If thou ask the truth, silence—silence." Then they brought a stick, and the tortoise seized the middle of it firmly in his teeth; and the ducks, taking up the two ends of it, carried him off. When they got to a height in the air, their way lay over a certain village; and the men of the village, getting a knowledge of it, were astonished at their appearance, and coming forth to admire it, set up a shout, to left and right, saying, Look at the ducks, how they are carrying a tortoise. And as the like of that appearance had never, in those days, reached the observation of that tribe, their shouts and screams kept increasing every moment. The tortoise, for some time, continued silent; at last the cauldron of her pride began to boil, and, her power of endurance being bowed down, she said, *Verse*—"Then let him be blind, every one that cannot see." But to open his lips, and to fall to the ground, was one and the same thing; and the ducks exclaimed, "Nothing belongs to a messenger but to arrive." It is laid on friends to give counsel; and on the fortunate to listen to advice. *Fragment.*—"Well-wishers give advice; but it is the fortunate, or well-disposed, who become susceptible of advice: my advice, although I am thy well-wisher, on thee, ill-fated, when shall it make an impression?"

And the use of the fable is this,—that every one who does not listen with an ear of consent to the counsels of his friends, will have laboured in his own destruction, and will have drawn the veil of advice from the features of his own ignominy. *Couplet.*—"That man who does not give ear to the words of the venerable, shall frequently bite the finger of shame."

The male Tītū said, I have listened to this example, that you have brought forward, and become well acquainted with its meaning; but do not fear, only keep your place; for men of weak hearts, who are timorous, never attain their object. My opinion is still the same; the envoy of the ocean will consider a regard for us among his bounden duties. So the female laid her eggs; and when the young ones, bursting out of the white shirt of the egg, put their heads forth from the collar of life, the sea, rising into waves, took them under the skirt of destruction. The mother, on beholding this catastrophe, fell into agitation, and said, O wretch! I knew there was no joking with the water; now thou hast given my children to the wind, and set my soul on fire: think at least of some contrivance by which some ointment may be laid upon my lacerated feelings. The male replied, Thou speakest words of dishonour; for acquitting myself of the obligation of my words, according to that very promise of mine, which thou knowest, I will obtain justice against the envoy of the ocean. He immediately repaired to the other birds; and collecting together into one place, all those, each and every one, who were the leaders and chieftains of each species, he fully explained his condition to them; and, beseeching their aid and succour, he began, in a voice of supplication, this song: *Couplet.*—"The details of the wretchedness of my heart are boundless: this is the season of succour, and the time of favour." If my honourable friends are not all of them, in this emergency, of one back and one heart; if they do not, with one accord, avenge me of the envoy of the ocean, his boldness will increase, and hereafter he will form a design against the young of other birds; and when this rule has become habitual, and this custom has received confirmation, you may as well tear up your hearts from your children, and bid farewell to your home and abode. *Couplet.*—"We must either, by a hundred insults, work his sorrow with disgrace; or turn our steps into the dismal abode of dissolution."

The birds, being much agitated and afflicted by this occurrence, wove their wings within each other; and hastening off to pay their duty at the court of the Sīmurgh, they carried the form of the event to the goal of representation, and said, If thou dost feel the griefs of thy subjects, thou art fit to be their sovereign; but, if thou hast no care for the sufferings of the afflicted, and no sorrow for the oppressed, then the inscription of sovereignty over the birds being erased from the page of thy prosperity, the patent of their guardianship shall be transferred to another. *Couplet.*—" Take care that thou feel the sufferings of the miserable; or tremble at the violence of fortune."

The Sīmurgh, kindly complying, set off with his servants and guards, from the abode of royalty, to repel this aggression; and the birds, with his help and succour, being strong in courage, turned their faces to the shore of the Indian ocean. And when the Sīmurgh, with an army, the extent and limits of which could not be contained within the extent of the reckoning of any accountant, and the number of their armies and species, the balance of surmise and possibility could never weigh. *Fragment.*—" All were audacious, fierce, valiant, and blood drinkers; all were courageous, experienced in war, and working vengeance; they had thrown over their breasts, mail and armour of feathers and wings; and had drawn out spears and daggers of claws and beaks." When he arrived in the neighbourhood of the ocean, the breeze of the dawn, which sets the long line of the waves in motion, carried the tidings to the envoy: and he, when he did not find within his own capacity strength to contend with the Sīmurgh and the army of birds, entering, of necessity, into a position of apology, restored the children of the Tītū.

And my purpose in relating the fable is this: That we ought not to despise any enemy, though he should be ever so feeble; for some work may be done by a diminutive needle, to which the lofty spear is incompetent: and a burning stick from the fire, though it appear small in our sight, yet will it burn whatever comes in contact with it. And philosophers have said, that the friendship of a thousand people is not to be put in comparison with the enmity of one person. *Couplet.*—" For friendship, a thousand persons are too few: for enmity, one would be a great number."

Shanzabah then said, I will not take the first step in the battle; that I may not be stamped with the infamy of ingratitude for favours: but as soon as the lion makes an attack upon me, I shall consider self-preservation, and the defence of my person, as incumbent. Damanah said, when thou goest near the lion, and seest that he has raised himself up, and is lashing his tail on the ground, and that the flame of his anger, like the fire of his eyes, appears to be kindled; be assured, that he has a design against thee. Shanzabah replied, If anything of this nature should appear, without a doubt, the veil of suspicion being withdrawn from the features of certainty, there will be conviction on the point of the perfidy and designs of the lion. Damanah, then rejoicing, and fresh in spirits, came back to Kalīlah. *Couplet.*—" The fool, whose joy is from the sorrow of others, seek not truth or honesty from him, for he is alienated from all."

Kalīlah said, How far are matters come? and, in what has the business concluded? Damanah gave answer, *Verse.*—" I am thankful for my own fortune; and also for the times." And God be praised, that the fullest relief has presented itself; and that such a difficult matter has been accomplished with success and ease. Damanah was saying this, while fortune, in the language of retribution, was whispering the purport of this couplet, in the ears of the wise men of the assembly of penetration. *Couplet.*—" The guests joyfully seized the ringlets of the cup-bearer: if heaven would but permit them to possess any security."

So they both went to the lion; and it so fell out that the ox came in immediately on their footsteps. The eyes of the lion fell on the ox; and the insinuations of Damanah coming into operation, the lion began to roar, and kept lashing the tail of assault on the ground, and was grinding his teeth with excess of rage. Shanzabah made sure that the lion had a design against him, and said to himself, The service of princes, in fear and consternation, and attendance upon kings, dread and terror, are like living in the same house with a snake, and dwelling in the same shelter with a lion: for though the snake may be asleep, and the lion hid, yet at last the former will raise up his head, and the latter will open his mouth. *Couplet.*—"Do not pay your court to kings, for I am afraid of it; lest it become suddenly like the intimacy of the stone and the pitcher." While thus reflecting he began the fight: and on each they perceived the signal which the impudent Damanah had described; and the battle being begun, they spread their roaring and bellowing through the whole space of the land, and the expanse of time. *Fragment.*—"From their uproar, the gentle and the ravenous beasts, in that plain and wilderness, were confounded: one took shelter in the cleft of a mountain; and another hid himself beneath the rubbish."

Kalīlah, observing this event, turned round to Damanah, and thus addressed him: *Quatrain.*—"Thou hast, with artful skill, stirred up a hundred stratagems; and then thou hast fled from the midst of the affair. The rain of two centuries will not allay this dust of calamity which thou hast raised." O fool! dost thou see the evil of the result of thine own proceedings, or no? Dost thou recognise the disgrace of the conclusion of thine undertaking? Damanah said, What is the evil result? The other said, This work which thou hast done; in this affair there are seven manifest evils: the First is this, that, without necessity, thou hast involved the master of thy prosperity in difficulty, and hast brought heavy trouble upon the spirit of the lion: the Second, that thou hast incited thy master so far, that he is become notorious for breach of promise and perfidy, and thou hast made this bad character to be his due: the Third, without any cause thou hast laboured for the blood of the ox, and hast thrown him into a pathless desert of destruction: Fourth, thou hast laid on thine own neck the blood of this innocent creature, who will be killed by thy exertions: Fifth, thou hast made a multitude evil-minded towards the king, and it is possible that, for fear of him, deserting their native land, they may repair to another; and wandering from their home, they may sink under the difficulties of foreign travels, and emigration from their native land: Sixth, thou hast rendered the chief of the armies of beasts an object of ruin, and the bond of their union will hereafter be left disjointed: Seventh, thou hast displayed thine own incompetency and weakness, and thou hast not carried to an end that boast. I will acquit myself of this business with mildness and gentleness. And surely he is the most stupid of mankind, who awakens strife that was asleep: and some undertaking which would admit of being pursued by peace and good will, he wishes to carry it on by quarrels and fierceness. Damanah said, Thou hast perhaps never heard how they have said, *Couplet.*—"The affair that does not succeed by wisdom, something of madness should be used in it." Kalīlah replied, In this affair, what point hast thou settled by the aid of prudence? or what plan hast thou formed by the help of the architect of deliberation, which not advancing, there was need of severity and harshness? After all, dost thou not know that sound judgment and righteous thoughts are preferred before audacity and bravery? *Verse.*—"Judgment is before the bravery of the bold." *Couplet.*—"A thoroughly wise man, with a word, performs works which are not to be accomplished by a hundred desolating armies." And thy admiration and infatuation about thyself; how thou art deluded by the pomp of this deceitful world, which, like the thick vapour of the desert, has nothing in it but an outward appearance, have always been known to me; but I felt a little hesitation about laying it open, as to whether thou would take any warning; whether thou wouldest arise, alert and vigilant, from the sleep of pride, and the insensibility and intoxication of the drink of conceit. But as thou hast now gone beyond all bounds, and art becoming, each moment, more wild and distracted in the desert of error and the pit of desperation, it is time that I should set forth a little of the height of thy ignorance and darkness, and of the excess of thy boldness and contumacy; and that I should recount a few of thy offences in words, and sins in conduct, though it may be but as a drop out of the ocean, or a grain of dust from a mountain. *Verses.* —"That thou mayest know what things thou hast done: drawing a pattern of perfidy, thou hast committed an error. On all points, thou art nothing in any account that is taken: though all others are something, thou, in short, art nothing."

Damanah said, O brother, from the beginning of life till this time, I do not believe that a word which was not fit, or an action was not suitable, has come into existence from me; yet if thou hast observed any fault in me, certainly it is right to set it forth. Kalīlah said, Thou hast many faults. The first is this; that thou fanciest thyself to be faultless: another, that thy talk preponderates over thy doings: and they have said, that there is no danger to a king equal to this, that the words of his ministers are weighter than his actions. And the men of the world are, as to words and actions, of four classes: First, there is the man who says and does not; and this is the habit of hypocrites and misers: Secondly, he who does not say, but yet does; and this is the practice of upright generous men: the Third, is one who says and does; which is the temper of men of society: and the Fourth is, he that neither says nor does; and this is the character of the base and low-minded. Now, thou art of that class which will talk, but do not adorn their words with the ornament of action; and I have always found thy talking far beyond thy merits. And the lion, deluded by thy narrations, is become exposed to such peril as this: and if, God protect us! any injury should befal him, anarchy and confusion will arise in these dominions; the misery and destruction of the people will exceed all bounds; all their lives and property will fall into danger of destruction and plunder; and the sin of all this misery will be upon thy neck. *Fragment.*—"Whoever is evil in action, or evil in thought, where shall he ever again see the face of welfare: whoever plants a sprig of injury, where shall he pick the fruit of benefit?"

Damanah said, I have always been a minister, giving good advice to the king; nor have I planted any but the shrubs of good counsel in the garden of his circumstances. Kalīlah replied, The shrub, whose fruit is that conduct which is now seen, had been better plucked up by the root: and that advice, which produces such consequences as have now come to sight, had been better, neither uttered nor heard. And how can any advantage be looked for in thy discourse, while the fact is that it is not adorned with the ornament of practice? For knowledge, without practice, is like wax without honey, it has not the least flavour; and talking, without doing, is like a tree without leaves or fruit, it is fit for nothing but to burn. *Verses.*—"Knowledge, which has no sign of being put in practice, is a carcase only, and there is no soul in it. Knowledge is a tree, and conduct is the fruit to it; it is especially for the sake of the fruit, that the tree grew up. The branch, which is without fruit, is hateful; it is a supply for the fire of the cooks."

And eminent men have, with the pen of kindness,

inscribed this upon the pages of their volumes; that from six things no advantage can be derived:—the First, discourse without practice; the Second, wealth without prudence; the Third, friendship without experience; the Fourth, knowledge without virtue; the Fifth, alms without pious intentions; and the Sixth, life without society. And the king, though in his own nature he be just and seldom oppressive, yet a minister, ill-disposed and of sordid character, will cut off all the benefits of his justice and clemency from all the people; and from dread of his opposition, the sorrowful tale of the afflicted never attains to the honour of being laid before the king; just like sweet and limpid water, in which the figure of a crocodile may be observed, no thirsty swimmer, though he may be excessively parched, can either open his hand in it, or place his foot in it. *Couplet.*—" I am come, parched to the liver, to a fountain of water; but what is the use; since there is no power to drink."

Damanah said, I had no object in this proceeding, but the honour of attending upon the king, Kalīlah said, Accomplished attendants, efficient servants, and ministers, who understand business, are the pride and ornament of the courts of kings: but thou art desirous that others should be set aside from doing their duty to the king; and that thou mayest be the one relied upon, and pointed out; and that high favour in his presence shall be confined to thyself; and this notion is from the extreme of ignorance, and the excess of folly; for princes are not to be restrained to any one thing or person. And the rank of sovereignty has a resemblance to grace and beauty; for just as some fascinating beauty, the more numerous her lovers, the more frequent is the display of the splendour of her attractions; so a king also, whatever number of servants and retainers may appear, his inclination will be for an addition to his retinue and attendants. And this unripe desire that thou hast, is a clear demonstration of excess of stupidity; just as philosophers have said, the signs of folly are five things:—First, to seek our own benefit in the injury of others; Second, to hope for the rewards of a future life, without holiness and charity; Third, to make love to women with harsh language and violence of temper; Fourth, to learn the subtle points of the sciences, with self-indulgence and ease; Fifth, to expect friendship from men, without faithfulness or regard to the rights of attachment. And it is from the height of that affection which I entertain, that I speak these words: or else it is as clear as the sun, that the dark night of thy depravity will never be made light by the torch of my preaching; and that the darkness of ignorance, and the blackness of envy, which are interwoven in thy being, will never be dissipated by the rays of my counsels. *Couplet.*—"It would not be possible, with the water of the well of Mecca, or the streams of Paradise, to bleach the blanket of the fortune of that man, which they have woven black." And the example of myself, with regard to thee, is the same as that of the man,* who kept saying to the bird, do not take fruitless trouble, nor waste thy words upon a set, who are not in a case to listen: but he would not attend, and in the end the just reward of it reached him.

Damanah enquired how it was, and Kalīlah told this

STORY.

They have related that a flock of monkeys held their abode on a certain mountain, and lived upon the fruits and herbs of it. By destiny, on a certain night, more black than the hearts of sinners, and darker than the minds of men of desperate fortunes, the army of winter made an assault upon them; and by the gust of the blasts of intense cold, the course of the blood in their bodies began to congeal. *Verses.*—"By the frost, the lion of the firmament was in hopes that he might change

* NOTE.—From the Story, it appears that it was not a man, but another bird, who said this to the bird. There is some mistake.

his skin, inside out, on his body: and in the fields, the birds had their shoes in the fire, (*i. e.* were in restless haste) for cheerfully would they be put on the spit to the fire. The poor creatures, distressed by the cold, were seeking some shelter; and in their search for it, girding themselves with alacrity, were running about into every corner. On a sudden, they saw a bright lump of quicksilver lying on one side of the road; and under a belief that it was fire, having collected some sticks and laid them about it, were blowing their breath on it. And opposite to them, a bird on a tree kept calling out, it is not fire: but they paid no attention, and did not desist from their fruitless task. By chance, in this interval, another bird came there and said to this bird, do not take this trouble, for they will not be hindered by thy talking, and thou wilt become vexed. *Couplet.*—" Every one who becomes allied to misfortune, in the commencement of his affairs, renounce him, for he will not become fortunate by perseverance." And to show any exertion in polishing and regulating such persons, is like trying a sword upon a stone; or to seek from deadly poison the properties of a sovereign antidote. *Fragment,*—" Whoever, in his origin, turned out base in nature, do not entertain a hope of any goodness from him. Because, assuredly, with every exertion, it is not possible to make, out of a black raven, a white hawk." When the bird saw that they did not listen to his words, from the excess of his kindness he alighted from the tree, in order that he might more clearly bring his advice to their ears; and make some remonstrance with them against that unprofitable labour which they were bearing, when the monkeys, collecting together about her, separated her head from her body. Now, my proceedings with thee have just the same character; I am wasting my time, and uttering unprofitable words: and whilst no benefit will result to thee, there is a fear also of some injury to me. *Fragment.*—" If the listener does not agree to thy counsel; why shouldest thou lay a useless burthen on thy tender heart. Thou hast said thus, mount the holy beast of happiness; that thou mayest reach unto the halting place, and thou mayest be free from care. But he would not hear; and goes on, just as before, in his way: let him alone, that, on foot, he may lag behind for his folly."

Damanah said, My brother! eminent men have always observed the conditions of integrity towards inferiors in their advice and counsel; and have abstained from their own inclinations and from deceit: and the maintenance of the usages of counsel and advice, is incumbent upon men of excellence; whether a person will listen to them, or will not. *Fragment.*—" Keep not thy advice from any person back, but speak; though there may be on the part of the hearer, some fault. The cloud does not withhold the drops of rain from the mountain; although it does not make any impression upon the heart of the marble."

Kalīlah said, I do not close the gate of advice against thee; but I am afraid of this, that thou hast laid the foundations of thy conduct upon deceit and stratagem, and hast taken self-opinion, and self-will for thy trade: " it is the worst qualification, that obstinacy:" and when thou shalt become ashamed, shame will do no good; and ever so often as thou shalt bite the back of thy hand, or scratch the face of the bosom, it will yield no profit. For every project, of which the foundations are built upon fraud and perfidy, the result of it will finish in disgust, and conclusion of it in disgrace. Just as it befel the cunning partner; and the evil of his stratagem turning into the ring of a snare of calamity, hung about his own neck: while the wise partner, by the blessing of honesty and a pure heart, attained his object.

Damanah asked the particulars, and Kalīlah said,

Story.

They have related that there were two partners; the

one prudent, the other negligent. The former, by the excess of cunning and counterfeit, would work a thousand changes upon the water; and men used also to call him Sharp-wit: the other, from the extent of his stupidity and ignorance, could not make any distinction between profit and loss; and him they called Light-heart. They had a claim upon a certain merchant; so, in union with each other, they set their faces to the journey, and went on folding up their stages and marches. By destiny, they found a sum of money on the way; and reckoning it great spoils, they began to hesitate. The clever one said, Brother, in this world, there is much profit, that is never made: at present, to be content with this sum, and to pass our days with tranquility, in the corner of our own hut, appears best. *Verses.*—"How long wilt thou wander about the world for the sake of gold? the more the gold becomes, the greater the sorrow grows. The cup of the eye of the avaricious was never filled. While the oyster shell was not satisfied, it was not filled with pearls." So they turned back; and being come near to the city, they alighted at the halting place. The inconsiderate partner said, come on! that we may divide this money; and getting free from alarm, may each of us spend our own share in whatever we like. But the clever one answered, At present, it is not expedient to make a division; the right course would be in this; that we should carry away that amount, for which necessity may occur for our expences; and let us lay the rest as a deposit some where, with great circumspection: and every certain number of days, coming, and taking from it, in proportion to our necessities, we will, in like manner, make the remainder secure; that it may be the further from danger, and the nearer to safety. The stupid partner, inveigled by the delusion, and receiving his fictions with approbation, they took, in the way that has been mentioned, a quantity of coin, and by agreement buried the remainder under a tree, and setting their faces towards the city, each took up his abode in his own home. *Couplet.*—"Next day, when the juggling sphere opened the lid of the chest of fraud," That partner who used to pretend to cunning, went to the foot of the tree, and taking all the pieces of money out of the earth, carried them away. The careless partner, knowing nothing of the matter, was busy in spending the cash that he had, till the least of it was not left. So he came to the clever one, and said, come along! and let us fetch something from our buried store, for I am grown completely destitute. The cunning fellow, pretending ignorance, said, it would be right. So they both came along together to the foot of the tree; but by how much the more they sought, the less did they find. Then Sharp-wit laid his hand on the collar of Light-heart, saying, this money thou hast taken, while any other person had not information. And the poor fellow, with all the oaths that he swore, and the lamentations that he made, did not reach his point. And to go on with the Story, their business went on, from a quarrel to a law-suit; and from a contest it terminated in an appeal. The cunning partner, bringing the careless one before the judge, made his claim upon him, and conveyed to the ear of the judge the purport of the Story, and the meaning of the dispute: and after the denial of Light-heart, the judge demanded from Sharp-wit, some proof in conformity with his claim. Sharp-wit said, "O Kāzī, may God Almighty preserve thee." *Couplet.*—"Take enjoyment of thy life; for on the bench of justice, all the sentences of thy life are stamped for perpetuity." There is no witness for me, with the exception of that tree, at the foot of which the gold was buried; and I hope that the Lord, glorious and almighty, by His perfect power, may bring that tree to speech, that it may establish evidence to the theft of this iniquitous traitor, who has carried off the whole of the cash, and made me desolate. The Kāzī was amazed at these words; and after a good deal of altercation and abundant talk, they gave rest to it upon this,—that next day, the Kāzī appearing at the foot of the tree, should call upon the tree for evidence; and that if its evidence should be conformable to the claim, he should upon its evidence make a decree. The cunning partner went home; and having detailed the whole affair to his father, withdrew the veil from the business, and said, And with a confidence in thee, my father, I have formed a notion of evidence from the tree; and with hopes in thee, I have planted the shrub of stratagem in the court of justice, and the whole project is connected closely with thy love; if thou wilt act in concert, we may carry off that gold, and obtain as much more, and pass the rest of our life in comfort and ease. The father said, What can that be, which depends upon me in this undertaking? The son said, The inside of the tree is hollow, in such a manner, that if two persons should be hid in it, one could not see them. It is necessary for thee to go this night, and to remain inside the tree till to-morrow, when the Kāzī shall come and call for evidence: then, as the custom is, thou canst bring thy testimony to fulfilment. The father said, My son! depart from the thought of fraud and stratagem; for if thou shouldst delude the creatures, thou canst not deceive the Creator. *Quatrain.*—"The Lord of heaven knows all thy secrets; for He knows thee, hair by hair, and vein by vein. I grant that, by fraud, thou mayest deceive mankind: What wilt thou do with Him? for He understands all things individually." Oh! many is the stratagem which has become a plague to its author; and the fit reward of it reaching even to himself, he has become disgraced and exposed. And I am fearful that, (let it not be), thy stratagem may be like the stratagem of the frog.

The son asked how that was, and the father said,

STORY.

They have related, that a frog had made her home by

the side of a snake, and had taken up her dwelling in the neighbourhood of that blood-sucking oppressor: and every time that the frog used to bring forth young, the snake used to eat them up; and used to afflict her heart with the brand of the loss of her offspring. This frog had an intimacy with a crab; one day she went to him and said, Obliging friend! think of some suitable scheme for me; for I have a superior enemy and a powerful foe; for neither to stand against him can be conceived, nor is any tale or allegory of vengeance within my reach. For the spot which I have made my dwelling, is a sweet place; and my delightful abode is a meadow, the dark green limits of which exhilirate the soul like the gardens of paradise; and its delightful breezes are perfumed, like the ringlets of beauties. *Verses.*—" A hundred thousand flowers are blown in it; the verdure is lively, and the water tranquil in it. Each flower of a different kind, in its colouring; the odour of each flower had extended a league. The volumes of roses had unfolded a hundred leaves; and the tulips held on their palms, cups of moisture. By the fragrance of the northern breeze, shedding odours, all the sides of it became mingled with perfume." And no person would by choice abandon such a residence; nor withdraw his heart from this specimen of the celestial paradise. *Couplet.*—" My abode is the street of the pagons; and what a lovely spot it is: no reasonable man in the world would abandon such a place."

The crab said, Do not suffer sorrow; for it is possible to bind a strong enemy in the noose of stratagem; and one can cast a superior foe into the snare of fraud. *Couplet.*—" If any one scatter the grains of stratagem, he may bring plenty of cunning birds into the snare."

The frog said, And in this chapter, what hard question of the book of subtlety hast thou solved; and what remedy hast thou got hold of, for the repulse of the evil of this malevolent enemy? The crab said, In a certain spot there is an ichneumon, fond of battle, and sharp tempered: catch a few fishes, and drag them, and spread them along, from before his hole, all the way to the dwelling of the snake: and so, as the ichneumon eats them up, one by one, and goes on in search of another, doubtless, when he comes to the hole of the snake, he will make use of him too; and will set thee free from his malice and mischief. The frog, by this contrivance, which coincided with destiny, destroyed the snake. When a space of two or three days had passed after this occurrence, there arose to the ichneumon a temptation to this, that he would make a movement in seeking to eat fish; and repeat the same scene to which he had now formed a habit. Again he set off, in search of fish, on the same road which he had before measured with the foot of desire; and as he found no fish he ate up the frog and her young ones. *Couplet.*—"Thou hast snatched me from the fangs of the wolf; but when I looked, in the end, thou thyself wast the wolf." And I have brought this example, because the termination of stratagem is entanglement; and the end of fraud and perfidy is shame and humiliation. *Couplet.*—"Set not thy foot in the valley of deceit and devices; for thou wilt fall into the snare of calamity, in the conclusion."

The son said, My father, shorten the discourse, and hold these far and distant thoughts in suspense; for this is a matter of little harm and much benefit. A lust for the money, and affection for his child led the helpless old man from the halting place of honesty and religion, to the deserts of violence and treachery; and the secret of "verily your wealth and their children are a temptation for you" came to publicity. Leaving the road of manliness untrodden, and entirely rolling up the carpet of fine feeling, he thought fit to undertake such a part, as in law and custom is forbidden and denied; and on that dark night, with a darkened heart took his place inside the tree. At dawn, when the clear minded Kāzī, the sun, became manifest on the judgment seat of the sky, and the perfidy of the black faced night became as clear as day to the creatures of the world;—the Kāzī, made his appearance with a concourse of eminent persons, at the foot of the tree; and the people, in a crowd to behold the sight, drew up in a line. The Kāzī, turning his face to the tree, after explaining the claim of the plaintiff, and the denial of the defendant, called upon it to explain the state of the case. A voice came forth from inside the tree, that Light-heart took away the money; and has done violence to Sharp-wit, who is his partner. The Kāzī was astounded; and by his sagacity understood, that some one was concealed within the tree; and that to expose him would not be attainable, but by an adroit contrivance. *Couplet.*—" The secret of every device which is hidden from the eye of prudence; except in the mirror of contrivance does not become manifest."

Then he gave orders; and so, collecting a great deal of rubbish, they laid it all about the tree, and set it on fire; till they brought smoke out of the family (or breath out of the body) of that unfinished man, raw business. The covetous old man, having a little while shewn patience, when he saw that the matter was come to his life, called for quarter: and the Kāzī, having extricated him and shewn him kindness, put questions to him about the truth of the case. The half-burnt old man revealed with truth the form of the event; and the Kāzī, being fully informed of the particulars, set forth to the people the characteristic of integrity and moderation in Light-heart, and the treachery and worthlessness of Sharp-wit. And coincident with this state of things, the old man, with his hypocrisy, removed the furniture of life from this perishable world to the mansions of eternity: and with all the heat of worldly fire, he found a union with the raging of the flames of futurity. The son, after he had met with the utmost chastisement, and had endured grievous severity, laying his dead father upon his neck, set off for the city. And Light-heart, by the blessing of righteousness and integrity, truth and probity, getting back his own money, became engaged in settling his affairs. And the conclusion from the recital of this example is this; that it may be known to mankind, that the results of deceit are unpleasant, and the conclusion of treachery is unhappy and contemptible. *Verses.*—"Whoever places his foot in the straits of deceit; at length will give his own head to the wind. Fraud is a snake which has two heads; and each one has a different kind of danger. That end, if it make the enemy heart-sore, this brings mischief to its owner."

Damanah said, Thou hast imposed upon judgment the name of deceit; and given to arrangement the epithet of fraud and perfidy. I have performed this object by sound arrangement, and have accomplished so great a matter with a right judgment. Kalīlah said, Thou art, in weakness of judgment, and infirmity of plan, in that state that the tongue becomes incompetent to the recital of it; and in baseness of mind, and violence of love for power, art at such a stage, that description is left at a loss in telling it. The advantage of thy fraud and deceit to thy master and the lord of thy prosperity, may be what thou seest: still at last, what will be the evil and the punishment of it with regard to thyself; for the infamy of thy double face and double tongue will yield an evil consequence. Damanah said, What is the harm of having a double face? for the beautiful rose is an ornament to the garden, from having a double face. And what is the fear of being double tongued; for the pen of the secretary, with its two tongues, is the guardian of wealth and dominion: the sword which has only one face, (or edge) to drink blood is its office; but a comb, which has two faces, (sides) its resting place is the forehead of the lovely. *Fragment.*— "He drinks blood, like a sword, in this age; every one who is of one face and of one tongue, because he is of a a pure nature: but that man who is like a comb, with double face and double tongue, they will give him a place on their foreheads, because of his superiority."

Kalīlah said, Damanah, leave off this boasting. Thou art neither that two-faced rose, that in beholding thy beauty the eye becomes bright; but rather, that heart-vexing thorn, from which nothing but injury comes to mankind: nor yet that two-tongued pen, that thou shouldst give information to the government and the kingdom; but rather, that double-tongued snake, for the wound of thy tongue can be nothing but hurtful poison: indeed, the snake has an excess of virtue over thee; for, from one of his tongues comes poison, and from the other, the antidote flows; whilst in thee, poison pours out from both tongues, and neither has any trace or token of the antidote. And it is right, that when nothing but antidote is produced by the tongue of any one, on account of his friends, if, for his enemies some poison should appear, it may be fit: just as an eminent man has said. *Couplet.*—"The antidote and the poison are to me, on the tip of the tongue; the first shall be for my friends, and the other for my foes."

Damanah said, Pass on from rebuking me; for perhaps reconciliation may grow up between the lion and Shanzabah; and again the foundations of affection and concord may be confirmed. Kalīlah said, This speech, again, is out of the collection of those sayings which are mingled with impossibility: and thou, perhaps, hast never learnt that three things must be established, before the occurrence of three things; after which, the settling of those things is of the class of what is forbidden, and their firm position is of the chapter of impossibilities. First, The water of a fountain or conduit is so long pleasant, as it has not reached the sea; but when it has joined the ocean, pureness and sweetness may not again be expected from it.

Second, Union among relations will take place, so long as evil-disposed and wicked persons have not interfered among them; but after it, the interference of the wicked and the malevolent, it is not possible to expect agreement and concord from relations and connections. Third, The springs of society and intimacy will for such a time be pure, as they do not give to tale-bearers and mischief-makers any opportunity of speaking; but when double faced, double-tongued men have found an occasion for plausible talk between two affectionate friends, reliance cannot again be placed on their friendship. And, hereafter, if the ox should find escape from the paws of the lion, it is not possible that, by his gentleness and flattery, he should turn from his path, or shew any desire for reconciliation and confidence with him: or upon the supposition that the gates of intercourse should still be left open, there will be to each an apprehension of the other. *Couplet.*—"When a thread is broken, it may be tied again; but a knot will be left in the midst."

Damanah said, If I, relinquishing attendance on the lion, become a recluse in the corner of my cottage, and seizing with the hand of attachment the skirt of intercourse with thy virtues, draw the head of seclusion within the collar of retirement,—how might that be? Kalīlah said, Far be it, that I should again keep company with thee; or have any inclination for thy society; for I have always been alarmed at this close intimacy with thee; and in my heart I have always rejected thy familiarity. For the learned have said, that we ought to abstain from the society of the ignorant and the vicious; and shew attachment to the service of the wise and virtuous: since an union with men of vice and profligacy is like rearing a snake: for how much the more the snake catcher takes trouble in nursing it, after all, the flavour of venom will give out a smell from his gums. While waiting upon men of understanding and purity of morals is like the casket of the apothecary: for if nothing of the contents falls to any man, in the end, the odours of his perfume will give fragrance to the palate. *Verses.*—" Be like an apothecary; for by the side of him the gown becomes perfumed by his fragrance. How long, like the forge of blacksmiths, wilt thou give on every side smoke and sparks."

O Damanah! how can one have any hope of thy faithfulness and kindness; since against a king (who has made thee noble, honourable, confidential, and illustrious, to such an extent that, in the shade of his prosperity, like the sun, thou dost boast of rising higher; and that, by reason of attendance upon his heaven-like threshold, thou dost place the foot of boasting on the forehead of the polar stars;) thou hast thought such conduct allowable; and hast imagined the claims of all his bounty and grace to be nothing. *Couplet.*—" Neither for justice nor for thyself hast thou any shame; nor also any modest sense of manly feeling." And I, if I choose a distance of a thousand leagues from such a person, a noble understanding will hold me excused; and if I should renounce fellowship with such a worthless person, reason, our guide, will connect me with rectitude. *Fragment.*—" To break off intercourse with friends in appearance, is more agreeable; for absence is pleasanter than the presence of one who is not congenial: that companion, by whose society thy mind is not gladdened, distance, to a hundred leagues from such a companion, is sweeter." And just as boundless advantages belong to the society of the virtuous and the holy; so mischiefs without end belong to an intercourse with the ignoble and wicked: and the society of bad men makes an impression more quickly; and the evil of it becomes manifest in a little time. Therefore, he who is completely wise ought to form a friendship with wise men, approved in their life, speaking the truth, and sweet in temper; and should keep aloof from a companion, lying, treacherous, ill-natured, and profligate. *Verses.*—" As long as it is possible to close the door in the face of mankind, sit down alone in the chamber of retirement. It is right to gain a virtuous companion; for every black heart is not fit for society. I have a recollection of these words from a wise man, on whose pure soul be mercy, viz. with the foolish, every man who became intimate, by their intimacy at last, he became entangled. And whoever takes an unworthy friend, or strengthens himself by an ignorant friend, that happens to him, which happened to the gardener.

Damanah asked what that was, and Kalīlah said,

STORY.

They have related that there was a gardener; for a long time he had been engaged in different kinds of agriculture; and had spent his dear life in laying out gardens and pleasure grounds. He had a garden, the paradise-like borders of which, by the deliciousness of its shrubs, had thrown the dust of envy into the eyes of the garden of Aram; and by the freshness of its flowers and streams had fixed a scar of distraction on the bosom of the gardens of the palace of Bahrām: on its variegated trees the splendour of a peacock was apparent, and from its gold-painted flowers the the blaze of an imperial diadem was refulgent; the surface of the ground was resplendent, like the countenance of a beauty wearing ornaments; and the gales of the air were perfumed, like the cottage of a master-dealer in ambergris; the flourishing trees, with the quantity of fruit, like aged men with bent backs; while the fruit, trickling with lusciousness, like a heavenly sweetmeat ripened without the heat of fire; the colours of its vernal and autumnal fruits to an excess of delicacy, and the last degree of elegance; its apples, without evil, like the chins of silver-bodied heart-stealers, ensnared all hearts; and by their lovely colour, and exhilerating odour, had captivated a world of people. *Fragment.*—" They have compared the apple to the chin of a mistress; its colour grew red, and the whole face was lighted up in the garden: the apple is a lamp, shining from the tree; who has seen a lamp at the end of a branch, in the bright day?" The pear had suspended, at every branch, jugs of the water of life, with pitchers full of a delicious juice of sugar; and by the offer of a delicate preserve excited the inclination of the indolent without capital or profit. *Verses.*—"What shall I say in praise of the pear; for in sweetness and delicacy, it is so many bottles of fine sugar hanging from the branches." And the quince, clothed in wool, like philosophers who rise by night, with its yellow complexion, had put forth its head from the cage of the monastery of creation: and its dust-soiled face had awakened the grief-soiled hearts of lovers from affection to their moon-like loves. *Couplet.*—"The quince is yellow with the sun, and I am yellow with my love; he from the moon and the sun, and I from the love of my mistress." The golden ball of the orange, shining from among the green leaves, like the globe of the sun blazing from the azure sky. And the gilded censer of the citron was sparkling in the courts of the garden, with its tranquilizing perfume and exhilirating odours. *Verses.*—"Its pomegranates, smiling like the lips of the mistress of our heart, was to all parties as delicious as the lustre of her teeth. By way of experiment, the heavens, like a goldsmith, had cast the essence of rubies into the fire, (or the pomegranate.) When my reason would sing a description of the peach; my discourse upon it would appear moist and sweet: as yet, its life is not come to our lip, when the juice of beauty and delicacy exudes from it." On one side there was an incomparable fig; such that the hand of power had fixed the quality of its beauty, in conformity with "and the fig;" and had composed a rare sweetness out of fragrant herbs and fine sugar. On another side, a transparent grape, the details of whose perfection the pen of wisdom had drawn upon the illustrious page of "and in it we raised up grain and the grape;" lay swelling, like a moist blister on the palm of the green leaf. And on the edge of the beds, the golden balls of the melons, with green ringlets and fair cheeks, like a new moon, which shews its face from the horizon of the azure-coloured sky, burst forth in splendour. *Verses.*—" Each melon ball, which had grown green in it, carried off the ball from the fruits of Paradise: with a freshness of ringlets, in the form of its hair never was; breathing musk, musk never had that odour."

And the old villager had so much attachment to each tree, that he had none of the enjoyments of a father, and no solicitude about children; but passed his time in solitude in that garden. But the end of the matter was, that he got into a strait with the horrors of solitude; and became to the last degree melancholy with the dread of being alone, and without a companion. *Verse.*—" Roses and violets, and all things, are here; but there is no friend: what is the good of them?"

But to the Story. From grief at being alone, he came forth to ramble in the plain; and was taking a walk on the skirts of a hill, which, like the extent of the length of hope, the expanse of it was not susceptible of limit. By chance, a bear, foul-tempered, ugly in shape, disagreeable in appearance, and impure in nature, had also, on account of his solitary state, turned his face from the top of the hill to the bottom. And in the moment that they met, on both sides, by reason of being of like kind, the chain of affection came into motion; and the heart of the peasant was disposed to the companionship and society of the bear. *Couplets.*—" The merest atoms that are in this earth and heaven, are, to their own kind, like the straw and the amber: bodies of fire are attractive to bodies of fire; bodies of light also seek bodies of light: what is pure, those who are pure are fond of: and sorrow also, those who are dark draw to themselves. What is it that carries away vain persons? some vanity: and what is it that is pleasing to the wise? a wise man. Men of error draw fools after them; and all the rest are pleased with all the rest."

The inexperienced bear, seeing the flattery of the peasant, was completely attached to his society; and upon a little signal, laying the head at his feet, entered the Paradise-like garden: and by enriching and honouring him with all those delicious fruits, friendship became confirmed between them; and the roots of the shrub of affection found firmness in the piece of land of the heart of each. *Verses.*—"In the corner of the garden, they continued for a space; in the union of each other constantly delighted."

And whenever the gardener, from excess of weariness, would lay, in the shade of repose, the head of tranquility on the pillow of rest, the bear, from motives of love and affection, sitting at the edge of his pillow, would drive away the flies. *Verse.*—"I do not wish, moreover, that even a fly should cast a shadow on that lip." One day, the gardener, in his accustomed way, was gone to rest, and had fallen into sleep; and a great many flies being collected on his face, the bear was occupied in fly-driving; but as often as he used to drive the flies away, instantly they would return; and as he would hinder them on this side, they would make an attack on the other side. The bear was exasperated, and taking up a stone, to the amount of twenty mans, (about half a ton,) with the design that "I will kill the flies," he cast it on the face of the helpless peasant. To the flies, no injury occurred from the danger of the stone; but the old gardener became all the same with the dust. And hence our forefathers have said, that in all circumstances, a wise enemy is better than a foolish friend. *Couplet.*—"A wise enemy, though he be the grief of the soul, is better than a friend who is ignorant."

And I have quoted this Story for this; that friendship with thee yields just the same result, as if the head should be in a situation of destruction, or the breast should become a target to the arrows of calamity. *Couplet.*—

"The society of fools is like an empty kettle; which on the inside is destitute, and on the outside black."

Damanah said, I am not such a fool that I do not distinguish what is beneficial to my friend from what is injurious; or that I cannot make a distinction of his good from his hurt. Kalīlah said, I acknowledge this; that thou art not in folly at that degree; yet the dust of sinister views makes the sight of the mind dark and corrupt: it is possible that, on account of some selfish object, thou wilt abandon the part of thy friend, and wilt make ready a thousand unsatisfactory explanations as an excuse for it: just as in the matter of the lion and Shanzabah, thou hast stirred up all this perfidy, and still dost make pretension to a pure garb and a good disposition. And the example of thee with thy friends, is like the example of that merchant, who had said, "In a city where mice eat a hundred *mans* of iron, what wonder if a hawk should carry off a boy?"

Damanah said, how was that?

STORY.

Kalīlah said, They have related that a merchant, of small means, was going on a journey: by way of forethought, he put a hundred *mans* of iron in deposit, in the house of a friend; so that if any necessity should occur, making that a source of livelihood, he might give some stability to the thread of subsistence. After the merchant had brought his journey to a conclusion, and had once more arrived at the object of his endeavours, he became in want of the iron: but the friend who had taken it in trust, had sold the iron, and spent the price of it.

One day, the merchant went unto him to demand the iron. The trustee led him into the house, and said, "O sir! I had laid by that iron in security, in a corner, and made my mind easy; thoughtless of this, that in that corner the hole of a mouse is situated: and by the time that I became aware of it, the mouse had perceived the opportunity to be great spoil, and had entirely eaten the iron. The merchant answered, Thou sayest true; for mice have a great affection for iron; and their teeth have entire power over such a juicy and tender morsel. *Couplet.* —"To mice, mouthfuls of iron are, just like macaroni, a delight to the throat."

The trust-worthy and veracious man, was rejoiced at hearing these words; and said to himself,—"This stupid merchant is deluded by this speech, and has taken off his heart from the iron: there is not any thing better than this, that I should do him hospitality, and should display the fashion of personal exertions in the feast; so that a confirmation may arise to this affair." So he gave the gentleman an invitation to an entertainment; and said, *Couplet.*—"If to my hospitality thou wilt set thy foot in my cottage; thou wilt do me a kindness, and shalt place thy foot on my eyes."

The good man replied, "To-day an urgent engagement has occurred; but I give a pledge, that in the morning at dawn I will come back." So he came out of his dwelling; and carried away a son of his, and concealed him in his house. At day-break he presented himself at the gate of his host. The host, in a distracted state, loosened the tongue of apology, thus: O worthy guest! hold me excused; for ever since yesterday a son has been absent from me; and two or three times they have sounded a proclamation in the city and the environs; and I have not obtained any tidings of that lost one. *Couplet.*— "Jacob-like, bewailing, I make lamentations; saying, ho! ho! who has any tidings of the lost Joseph?"

The merchant said, Yesterday, as I was coming out of thy house, I saw a boy, just of the description thou sayest, whom a hawk had carried off, and taking her flight, was bearing him through the air. The trusty man uttered a cry, saying, Stupid fellow! why dost thou utter impossible words; and for what purpose dost thou charge a life of this enormity on thyself? A hawk, whose whole body cannot be half a *man;* how can she move, and carry into the air, a child which is of the weight of ten *mans?* The merchant smiled, and said, Do not be surprised at this. In a city, where a mouse is able to eat a hundred *mans* of iron, a hawk, too, is able to carry into the air a boy, who is ten *mans*. The trustee perceived how the case was, and said, Do not suffer grief, for the mouse has not eaten the iron. The merchant said, Do not be unhappy; for the hawk has not carried off thy son: give the iron, and take the boy.

And I have told the Story, that thou mayest know, that in a sect, where a man may shew perfidy to his benefactor, it is clear, what he can imagine with respect to others: and since thou hast done this to the king, there is not left, to others towards thee, a hope of fidelity, or expectation of discharging thy duty. And to me it is clear, that to keep away from the darkness of thy wickedness is necessary; and to abstain from the blackness of thy deceitfulness and treachery is essential. *Couplet.*— "The bonds of prosperity arose from cutting such a fellow as thee: the chief source of happiness is not seeing thy face."

When the conversation of Kalīlah and Damanah came to this point, the lion was at leisure from the affair of the ox, and had cast him into dust and gore. Yet, when the lion, with the claws of chastisement, had settled the matter of Shanzabah; and had cleared the space of the wilderness of his being; when the strength of his anger and the violence of wrath had received quiet—he fell into meditation, and said to himself, Alas! for Shanzabah, with such wisdom, and prudence, and judgment, and talents; I know not whether, in this business, I have drawn my breath in rectitude, moved my foot in error; nor whether in what they have brought to me about him, they have fulfilled the rights of honesty, or taken the road of treachery. I at least, have involved myself in calamity by reproaches; and with my own hand have made a faithful friend to taste the drink of destruction. *Couplet.*—" Can a friend with a friend, after all, do this; I am an infidel, if any infidel would do this."

The lion, casting down his head in remorse, and loosening the tongue of rebuke, kept blaming his own folly and hastiness; whilst the form of Shanzabah, in the language of the occasion, was bringing to his ears the meaning of this quatrain. *Quatrain.*—" O friend! does any one without cause, kill a friend? and even then, does he kill such a faithful friend as me? Do not call thyself a friend; take thyself as an enemy to me. Would any one so cruelly kill his enemy?"

The continual smile of the lion was, by sorrow for this event, changed into weeping: and his constitutional heat became twofold, by the burning of that occurrence. *Couplet.*—" The hand of thy departure has placed for me, the scar of sorrow in the breast; so that from this thorn of grief for thee, what flower shall again blossom?"

Damanah, as from a distance, saw the signs of compunction manifest on the forehead of the lion, and observed proofs of remorse on his front, breaking off the discourse of Kalīlah, went before him and said. *Verses.*—" O king! let the throne and prosperity be thy place; the throne of the sky be thy couch: may thy flourishing head be exalted in joy; and the head of thy foe cast at thy feet."

What is the cause of thoughtfulness, and what can be the reason of reflection? Where is there a time more joyful than this? or a day more blessed than this? When the king moves proudly in a station of victory and triumph; and his enemy is wallowing in the dust of contempt, and the gore of disappointment. *Couplet.*—" The dawn of hope has drawn the sword of triumph; behold! the day of the enemy is come to an evening of destruction: behold!"

The lion said, Every time that I recollect the polite manners in attendance, and the forms and effects of the wisdom and society, and the many kinds of accomplishment of Shanzabah, an agony becomes victorious over me; and grief and consternation get triumphant over me: and in truth, he was the support and defence of the army, and the power of the arm of valour used to increase to my followers, by his assistance. *Couplet.*—" He is gone; he, by whom the affairs of a world adds stability; he is gone; he, by whom the house of the kingdom was firm."

Damanah said, To the king there is no occasion for that despiser of his bounty, that traitor in practice; but rather for this victory, which has shewn its face, he ought to set forth daily portions of thanks to God; and for this triumph, which has given him the hand, he should open the gates of exultation and rejoicing in the precincts of his heart. *Couplet.*—" The dawn of triumph has arisen from the eastern horizon of hope; to men of sinister designs the night of madness is come to an end." You should reckon this auspicious record of victory, (by which the chronicles of prosperity are adorned); and this mandate of august success, (by which the register of happiness becomes ornamented); as an illustrious preface, and a sublime opening, to the pages of the times. *Fragment.*—" This day, good fortune brings me glad tidings; and to prosperity there are a hundred melodies, in the key of hope. It is a day, this, which my heart, with thousands of prayers, has sought; it is a period, this, which my soul, with thousands of wishes, has desired."

O king! O refuge of the world! To have pity upon a person, from whom one cannot be secure as to life, is an error: and to make the enemy of the king a prisoner in the confinement of the grave, is the act of the wise. The finger, which is the ornament of the hand, and the instrument of seizing and holding, if a snake should inflict a wound upon it, for the preservation of the rest of the body they cut it off; and they reckon the pain of that wound as the essence of ease. *Couplet.*—" What work can the enemy do, that thou shouldest make mention of him; it is better that thou make thy heart glad in the loss of him."

The lion, was a little soothed by these words. But fortune took just amends for the ox: at the conclusion of the affair, Damanah drew on to ignominy and disgrace; and the shrub of his bad actions, and the seed of his false words coming to fruit, he was slain in retaliation for the ox. And the consequences of fraud and deceit have always been hateful; and the conclusions of cunning and malevolence, despicable and unpropitious. *Verses.* —" The malevolent, even in his own project his head goes, like the scorpion, who seldom gets back to her home. If thou do evil, have no expectation of good: for the colocynth does not produce grapes for fruit. Do not fancy, O thou that hast sown barley in autumn, that thou shalt gather wheat in the time of harvest. A teacher spake a proverb, such as this:—do not evil, or thou shalt experience from fortune; that man shall see good in both abodes, who brings happiness to the people of God.